Undeserved

How God's grace can erase your failures

Mike Novotny and Bruce Becker

Published by Straight Talk Books
P.O. Box 301, Milwaukee, WI 53201
800.661.3311 · timeofgrace.org

Printed in the United States of America
ISBN: 978-1-949488-45-6

Contents

Introduction

True or false? The Old Testament is filled with stories of picture-perfect families, ideal marriages, textbook parenting, obedient children, and siblings who *always* show love to one another.

Not even close to true.

In fact, the Old Testament is jam-packed with stories of dysfunctional families, wrecked marriages, pathetic parenting, godless children, and cutthroat sibling rivalries. And these stories aren't just of the wicked and godless families living in Old Testament times. These stories often involve folks whom God had graciously called to be his special people.

Flawed is the word that comes to mind. Flawed families made up of flawed individuals living flawed lives.

If you crack open your Bible to Genesis, you will find an example of a flawed marriage already in the third chapter of the very first book of the Bible. The first couple, whom God personally created, ruined their lives (and ours). They destroyed the perfect relationship they had with God and with each other. And they did this even before they had kids. Then, when Adam and Eve had their first two sons, one son murdered the other in a fit of jealous rage. Flawed parents. Flawed kids. Flawed lives. And that was only the start of it.

Adam and Eve, along with all their descendants (you and me included) were definitely flawed. But they were also blessed. Despite the wreckage Adam and Eve caused for the human race in the Garden of Eden by disobeying God's clear command not to eat the fruit of the forbidden tree,

God came alongside of them immediately. He assured them of a plan to repair the relationship they once had with their Creator. God's plan would involve his own Son. At God's appointed time, the Son would leave heaven's glory, become a human being, and restore the broken relationship between God and us.

The New Testament book of Galatians sums up God's restoration and freedom plan: **"But when the right time came, God sent his Son into the world. A woman gave birth to him, and he came under the control of the laws given to Moses. God sent him to pay for the freedom of those who were controlled by these laws so that we would be adopted as his children"** (Galatians 4:4,5 GW). The "him" is Jesus.

In this book, we will explore the life of one of Adam and Eve's descendants who could very well be called the poster child for "flawed but blessed." His name was Jacob. He was the son of Isaac and Rebekah and the grandson of Abraham and Sarah. As we study the life of Jacob, I think you will come to realize that Jacob is a reflection each of us sees each day in the mirror. It shouldn't come as a surprise that you and I are a lot like Jacob—flawed, but also blessed.

This book is divided into two sections. In part one, Pastor Mike Novotny shares five stories from the life of Jacob. At the end of each story, there are a few questions for you to dig deeper and apply God's truth to your own life. In part two, I explore the life of Jacob in greater detail. I explore how Jacob's flaws and his blessings mirrored both his parents' lives as well as were inherited by his children.

Bruce H. Becker

Why Does God Love Me?

Mike Novotny

I bet you and I have the same problem—self-control, the rare ability to control ourselves. Self-control is the strength to say no, to wait, to be patient in the face of some short-term pleasure. I bet you're a lot like me. You know the right thing, the smart thing, the best thing to do, but . . . knowing and doing are two different things.

Like when I eat ice cream. I know I should put one scoop in a small dish. But I don't. I hold the whole pint in my warm hand, which melts the edges and lets me shovel 2,000 calories of Cow Tracks into my mouth in under five minutes. Or the snooze bar. I know I should get up, work out, pray, make a good breakfast. But I don't. That little rectangle is covered in fingerprints.

A lack of self-control is at the root of so much of our dysfunction.

But it gets more serious than that, right? A lack of self-control is at the root of so much of our dysfunction at home, at work, and at school. Most of us know we should be kind and selfless and gentle and patient and forgiving. But when your co-worker jumps to conclusions in the staff-wide email or your brother's big opinions get posted or announced at the family gathering or your girlfriend gives you that look . . . When your buddy is doing a snarky impression of everyone's least favorite teacher . . . When you're already feeling a buzz and the boys are buying another round . . . When you have to choose between your preferred to-do list and giving others your full attention, self-control is so hard.

But it's so good! The next day when you wake up without regret or shame or a spiritual hangover (or an actual hangover), there is joy on the other side of self-control. My pastor predecessor loved to say STP = LTP. Short-term pain equals long-term pleasure. The pain of saying no, of being self-controlled, leads to long-term pleasure, lasting joy.

Think of it like Jesus' food truck. Suppose Jesus and Satan both opened their very own food trucks. Every day they parked downtown, waiting for the hungry lunch crowd to come streaming out of their offices. Jesus quickly became famous for the best food in town. Fresh. Delicious. And, best of all, free. (Jesus is a pretty giving guy, you know.) But there was a catch. Jesus made everything from scratch. No microwaved meals. No thawing old meat. No layer of skin on top of the day-old cheese dip. Jesus' food was good, but you had to wait. And the lunch hour was, well, an hour. Which is what gave Satan such good business. Food would fly out of that little window fast. No lines. No wait. No patience required.

So how do we wait? Where does self-control come from? The Bible's answer to that question is interesting. And it's at the heart of a story from the book of Genesis. Genesis is primarily about one multigenerational, dysfunctional family, the family of Abraham, Isaac, and Jacob, a family with issues of sin and self-control. Yet in the middle of their story, we find the unexpected place where self-control is found.

Let's jump into their story in Genesis chapter 25:19-23:

This is the account of the family line of Abraham's son Isaac. Abraham became the father of Isaac, and Isaac was forty years old when he married Rebekah daughter of Bethuel the Aramean from Paddan Aram and sister of Laban the Aramean. Isaac prayed

to the Lord on behalf of his wife, because she was childless. The Lord answered his prayer, and his wife Rebekah became pregnant. The babies jostled each other within her, and she said, "Why is this happening to me?" So she went to inquire of the Lord. The Lord said to her, "Two nations are in your womb, and two peoples from within you will be separated; one people will be stronger than the other, and the older will serve the younger."

Rebekah was going to have twins. And from the start, these brothers fought. They jostled each other, duking it out for extra legroom in the womb. And after their births, they would grow into two nations, two separate nations (spoiler alert—the nations were Israel and its southeastern neighbor Edom). And the older twin would serve the younger.

That's an interesting promise. In our culture, we think of birth order as a personality thing, right? Firstborn = responsible Type A. Second born = goofy and attention-seeking. That theory came from psychologist Alfred Adler about one hundred years ago. But in this past culture, being the firstborn was way more important than that. The firstborn got two special blessings in that culture—money and power. He got the birthright, which gave him a double chunk of the inheritance money. And he got the blessing, which gave him power over the rest of the family who would serve and submit to him. We might think of it like the will and the power of attorney. God told Rebekah that the younger twin, the second born, would get the blessing, would have the authority, that the older would serve the younger. Apparently, the older would keep the birthright, the double inheritance. But—and here's the question—would either of them have the self-control to wait for God's promise?

We're about to find out. But first here's more on the twins:

When the time came for her to give birth, there were twin boys in her womb. The first to come out was red, and his whole body was like a hairy garment; so they named him Esau. After this, his brother came out, with his hand grasping Esau's heel; so he was named Jacob. Isaac was sixty years old when Rebekah gave birth to them. The boys grew up, and Esau became a skillful hunter, a man of the open country, while Jacob was content to stay at home among the tents. Isaac, who had a taste for wild game, loved Esau, but Rebekah loved Jacob. (Genesis 25:24–28)

The first baby comes out red and hairy. Really hairy. "His whole body was like a hairy garment." Out of curiosity, I googled "hairiest newborns" and had to show the entire office the results. That's Esau. Esau is a man of the open country. A guy with an F150 and a closet full of camo. A *Field & Stream* subscriber. A pack of Skoal in the back pocket of his Fleet Farm jeans. Esau seems to come from the Hebrew verb *Asah*, which means "to do." Esau is a doer. A guy who gets the job done. Who comes home from the woods with the kill.

But Jacob, the second twin, is not like Esau. Not at all like Esau. He is content to stay at home. Who wants to sleep in the woods when you have a nice tent at home? But don't diss Jacob as a weak momma's boy. He's smart. In fact, he comes out of the womb holding on to Esau's heel, trying to catch a free ride to freedom. They name him Jacob, which means "heel grabber." Someone who could trip you up. Esau can out-bench his baby brother, but Jacob can outsmart him any day.

And sadly, like too many families today, the differences divide them. The personalities and passions and strengths, instead of uniting the family like parts of a body, rip them apart in an ugly lack of self-control. That's how Genesis chapter 25 ends: **"Once when Jacob was cooking some stew, Esau came in from the open country, famished"** (verse 29). Classic. Esau in the open country. Jacob among the tents. Esau panting like an animal after the hunt. Jacob cooking stew while cooking up a plan. Esau impulsive. Jacob intelligent. Jacob's been waiting for this day, angry about his father's favoritism, hunting for his brother's birthright. He wants his money, and now is the time to get it.

> [Esau] **said to Jacob, "Quick, let me have some of that red stew! I'm famished!" (That is why he was also called Edom.)**
>
> **Jacob replied, "First sell me your birthright."** (Genesis 25:30,31)

In Hebrew, Esau's words are cavemanish. He says, "Make me swallow the red stuff! This red stuff!" He's not a smart man. But Jacob is: "First sell me your birthright."

Could you do that? About one hundred years ago, archaeologists stumbled upon some documents while digging around in Iraq that were four thousand years old. They called them the Nuzi texts. In the Nuzi texts, we find the story of two brothers who traded for a birthright. Tupkitilla wanted his brother Kurpazah's birthright. So he traded three sheep for the double portion of Dad's wealth.

But Jacob's offer to Esau isn't a good deal. Because their dad, Isaac, is loaded! Isaac's father, Abraham, left him his entire estate, and Abraham was loaded. In Genesis chapter 26,

Isaac will become so rich that the king of the Philistines will ask him to move far away so his massive flocks don't devour all of the grass in the country. This is like Warren Buffett's kid taking his name out of the will . . . for a bowl of soup.

But Esau's strength is not self-control.

"Look, I am about to die," Esau said. "What good is the birthright to me?"

But Jacob said, "Swear to me first." So he swore an oath to him, selling his birthright to Jacob.

Then Jacob gave Esau some bread and some lentil stew. He ate and drank, and then got up and left. So Esau despised his birthright. (Genesis 25:32–34)

"I'm dying!" impulsive Esau cries. "What choice do I have?" Esau thinks. (How about walking over to Mom and Dad's tent over there?) And Jacob trips up his impulsive brother: "Swear to me first. Swear to God. Sign on the dotted line." And Esau does. He eats. He drinks. He swallows. He burps. He leaves. He despises his birthright. End of chapter.

What's the moral of the sad story? The New Testament actually tells us in Hebrews 12:16: **"See that no one is sexually immoral, or is godless like Esau, who for a single meal sold his inheritance rights as the oldest son."** For a single meal, for something that would not satisfy, he sold something so precious. What does God want you to know? Don't sell something so good for something so small.

Have you ever heard of the Stanford Marshmallow Test? In the 1960s, a Stanford professor offered kids a choice— You can eat this marshmallow now or, if you can wait, you'll get two marshmallows later. And then the researcher left the room. Want to guess what happened? A few of the kids ate the marshmallow immediately! But most tried to wait. They *tried*. They covered their eyes. They turned around. They tugged on their pigtails. One kid petted the marshmallow like it was a stuffed animal. In the end, only 1 of 3 kids had the self-control to wait for the reward.

There is always a marshmallow, a way to get immediate gratification.

How do you think you would have done? Because, really, life is exactly like that except with the stakes raised. There is always a marshmallow, a way to get immediate gratification. There are words, actions, substances, and choices that give us pleasure, comfort, and a rush right now. And there are incredible rewards for waiting, way more than another marshmallow. But you have to wait way more than 15 minutes.

This is our test, right? The reformer Martin Luther once said, "Each of us is either an Esau or a Jacob." And the deceiver hopes you are a lot like Esau, because that's what the devil is, a deceiver. The word first shows up in Genesis 3:13, the fall into sin. Eve admitted, **"The serpent deceived me, and I ate."** The devil's go-to move is deception. He hopes we are as hungry as Esau. He wants us to believe we will die if we don't get this right now. He tries to make us think, "I have to. I can't live without this. I can't be happy without this." He makes the soup smell so good and the birthright seem so small.

So what's your soup? What do you want so badly you'd trade your blessing, your character, your faith to get it? Respect? You want to be respected. You want to be the athlete the coaches respect or the student with impeccable grades or the young star at your company or the parent whose kids can swim and swing and play piano. So you trade in the things that keep you close to God. You're too busy to gather for worship, have too much practice to go to Bible class, are too tired to spend time in God's Word each day, are too swamped to go and love people who don't know Jesus. But you find out their respect is hard to get and impossible to keep. Or maybe your soup is productivity. You get stuff done. You check the boxes. You work hard. But you're so focused, you don't see them. You rush past opportunities to listen, truly listen, and show compassion. You treat people—your own children—as interruptions and not opportunities. But you find out there's always more to do, always another box to check. Or maybe your soup is your image. You want to look good. So you zoom and crop and filter. You don't really confess your sins because your image would be trashed. You don't hang out with the poor, the broken, the unpopular. But you find out you can't control your image. People jump to conclusions. They see through the filters. And the deceiver trips you up again. You faith-plant into the dust of sin and realize too late, like Esau, that you lacked self-control.

So how do you change that? How do you learn to wait, to say no to short-term pleasure? How do you get more self-control? The Bible's answer is in a famous passage. Look at Galatians 5:22,23: **"The fruit of the Spirit is . . . self-control."** Self-control is fruit. It's not so much something you choose; it's something you grow. It's something that happens, that shows up when the Holy Spirit is working in your heart.

How does that all work? That's the interesting part. It's not counting back from 5 or taking a deep breath. The key to self-control is in Jacob's story too. It's the answer to this question: Why does God choose Jacob? Jacob is about to get a name change. God is going to call him Israel. God is going to grow him into a nation. God is going to make him the ancestor of Jesus. Why would God do that? Jacob is a heel grabber, a deceiver, and this soup thing is nothing compared to the sin that's coming! So why would God ever choose him, bless him, or save him? And the answer is in Romans 9:11-13. Check this out (this is huge!): **"Yet, before the twins were born or had done anything good or bad—in order that God's purpose in election might stand: not by works but by him who calls—she was told, 'The older will serve the younger.' Just as it is written: 'Jacob I loved.'"** Why did God love Jacob? Not because of Jacob's works. Not because he was such a great guy. No, because God is merciful. Because God elects and calls and chooses people who are flawed, who are broken, who are sinful.

In fact, God is so committed to loving you, choosing you, saving you despite your lack of self-control that he didn't change his Son's name. Did you know these days that some Christians are not using the name Christian? There are so many embarrassing Christians around they don't want to be associated with that, so they call themselves "Jesus Followers" or something. But here's what I love. Here's why I love Jesus. Jesus Christ didn't change his name. He didn't look at me and say, "If that guy is Christian, I don't want to be Christ. Call me Jesus the Nazarene or something." No, despite all my struggles, despite all our impatience, Jesus is not going to change his name. Look how Hebrews 2:11 says it: **"So Jesus is not ashamed to call them brothers and sisters."** He's not ashamed to admit the connection, not ashamed you are part of his family. If self-control is the fruit, Jesus is the soil.

Like Abraham and Isaac and Jacob, we are pretty dysfunctional people. But Jesus died for dysfunctional people, and Jesus rose from the dead to bless us with a born-again birthright, an inheritance in heaven. That is the soil where the fruit of self-control grows. When that gets in you—"I am already loved, already accepted, already respected, already valued, already secure, already rich in Christ"—then you don't have to go for what the devil is offering. "Soup? Satan, you're offering me soup? I already have peace, already have joy, already have everything I need. I have the Bread of Life. I have the Water of Life. I ain't Esau. I'm not dying. I'm alive in Christ! And I'm willing to wait for it."

I'm alive in Christ!

So remember Jesus. Remember the Son of Jacob who is not ashamed of you. Remember everything you already have in him, and you'll find growing, bit by bit in your heart, the fruit of self-control.

God's Truth for My Life

1. In what areas of your life do you lack self-control? Examine your words, actions, and thoughts and share your struggles with a close Christian friend.

2. Name three reasons why Jesus is the key to the fruit of self-control. What is it about Jesus that makes us willing to wait for God's will to be done in God's time?

3. List three ways your self-control is like "fruit." (For example, fruit is what comes from plants just like self-control is what comes from Jesus.)

Why Does God Love Liars?

Mike Novotny

If there's one thing soccer lovers and soccer haters can agree on, it's that lying is bad. And no one in the world lies more than professional soccer players. Ever seen a game? Nudge Brazilian superstar Neymar, and he will do a quadruple barrel roll and shriek like he's giving birth to twins. Bump Uruguayan forward Luis Suárez on the hip, and he'll grab his head like he's been pistol-whipped. But after the call, the gravely injured jump up at full sprint. There's more miraculous healing in a World Cup soccer game than at a revival service. So why do they do it? They hate it when the other team lies, so why do they lie? Because a lie gets you a call, and a call gets you a kick, and a kick can get you a goal. And why do goals matter? Because when you score more goals, you win the game. When you win the game, you get respect, fame, attention, money, power, praise, sex, and glory. That is why they lie.

And that is something we all can relate to. You know how you feel when someone lies to you or about you. But sometimes a lie is the only way to get something or not to lose something, something you really want.

A few examples—Think of facing Dad's question: "What did you do to your brother?" Tell the truth, and you're going to lose screen time, sleepover plans, or your parents' approval. Think of the interview question: "Why did you leave your last job?" Tell the truth, and you might not get the new job. Think of facing the judge's question: "How much have you been drinking?" Tell the truth, and you might lose the case or custody of the kids. Think of a spouse's question: "Why are we behind on the credit card?" Tell the truth about going out to eat and some Amazon one-clicks, and you might lose a peaceful night. Think of the customer service counter: "Did you wear the garment at all?" Tell the truth, and you might lose the $29.99 you paid. Think of the traffic stop: "Do you know how fast you were going?" Think of the high school conversation: "You don't like that loser, do you?" Think of the friends wanting you to corroborate their lie. Think of the teacher asking, "Why didn't you get the assignment done?"

This is what makes the truth so hard. The truth costs you. You might lose their respect, trust, approval, friendship, love. You might lose the promotion, the job, the relationship, your freedom. Which is why, in the moment, we don't tell the truth. We are very tempted to lie.

Their ugly story of lies reminds us why we shouldn't lie.

Which is why I need to tell you another story about Jesus' relatives, Jacob and Rebekah. Jacob is famous in the Bible for his lies, and he learned the art of lying from his mother, Rebekah. Their ugly story of lies reminds us why we shouldn't lie and why we all need Jesus, who is the Truth.

Let me take you back about four thousand years to the dysfunctional family of Isaac, Rebekah, and their twin sons, Esau and Jacob. Genesis 27:1-4 says:

> **When Isaac was old and his eyes were so weak that he could no longer see, he called for Esau his older son and said to him, "My son."**
>
> **"Here I am," he answered.**
>
> **Isaac said, "I am now an old man and don't know**

**the day of my death. Now then, get your equip-
ment—your quiver and bow—and go out to the open
country to hunt some wild game for me. Prepare me
the kind of tasty food I like and bring it to me to eat,
so that I may give you my blessing before I die."**

Ah, the blessing. In those days the blessing was a verbal,
legal, and binding way to give your authority to another person. The firstborn son would get the blessing, the responsi-
bility, and the authority to be lord of the family, to be served
by his brothers. And old Isaac wants to give the official,
notarized blessing to his firstborn, his favorite, Esau.

But what blind Isaac can't see is his wife, Rebekah,
eavesdropping on the conversation. Rebekah does not love
Esau like Isaac does. Esau is hairy and rugged and impulsive. He marries the women he wants, no matter what those
women worship. No, that's why she loves Jacob. And that's
why she comes up with a lie for Jacob to tell. "Quick," she
commands her son. "Esau is about to get the blessing. Get
two goats. I'll make Esau's famous recipe. You pretend to be
your brother, and Dad will give you the blessing!"

But Jacob hesitates, "Me? Esau? Mom, the second Dad
touches these smooth arms, he'll know I'm not Esau!"

But Rebekah grins, "Trust me." And he does. Jacob runs
to get the goats. Rebekah runs to get Esau's clothes. She
whips up some gourmet goat meat, wraps the hairy goat-
skins around Jacob's neck and arms, and pushes Jacob out
the door toward Isaac's tent.

Hold your breath with Jacob as you read what happens
next:

[Jacob] **went to his father and said, "My father."**

"Yes, my son," he answered. "Who is it?"

Jacob said to his father, "I am Esau your firstborn. I have done as you told me. Please sit up and eat some of my game, so that you may give me your blessing."

Isaac asked his son, "How did you find it so quickly, my son?"

"The Lord your God gave me success," he replied.

Then Isaac said to Jacob, "Come near so I can touch you, my son, to know whether you really are my son Esau or not."

Jacob went close to his father Isaac, who touched him and said, "The voice is the voice of Jacob, but the hands are the hands of Esau." He did not recognize him, for his hands were hairy like those of his brother Esau; so he proceeded to bless him. "Are you really my son Esau?" he asked.

"I am," he replied.

Then he said, "My son, bring me some of your game to eat, so that I may give you my blessing."

Jacob brought it to him and he ate; and he brought some wine and he drank. Then his father Isaac said to him, "Come here, my son, and kiss me."

So he went to him and kissed him. When Isaac

caught the smell of his clothes, he blessed him and said, "Ah, the smell of my son is like the smell of a field that the LORD has blessed. May God give you heaven's dew and earth's richness—an abundance of grain and new wine. May nations serve you and peoples bow down to you. Be lord over your brothers, and may the sons of your mother bow down to you. May those who curse you be cursed and those who bless you be blessed." (Genesis 27:18–29)

Doesn't your heart break for poor Isaac? He knows something isn't right. But without his sight, he only has four senses left. His ears tell him it's Jacob, but his nose smells Esau. His hands touch Esau, and his tongue tastes Esau's food, and who but Esau even knew about the meal? So his senses vote 3–1, and Isaac sides with the majority. He gives the blessing, the authority: "Be lord over your brothers."

Just then Esau comes in from the hunt, clueless. I imagine he is grinning, anticipating the most important moment of his life, whistling as he skins an animal and makes the meat just like Daddy likes it. Here's the ugly result of Rebekah and Jacob's lies:

He too prepared some tasty food and brought it to his father. Then he said to him, "My father, please sit up and eat some of my game, so that you may give me your blessing."

His father Isaac asked him, "Who are you?"

"I am your son," he answered, "your firstborn, Esau."

Isaac trembled violently and said, "Who was it, then, that hunted game and brought it to me? I ate it just before you came and I blessed him—and indeed he will be blessed!"

When Esau heard his father's words, he burst out with a loud and bitter cry and said to his father, "Bless me—me too, my father!"

But he said, "Your brother came deceitfully and took your blessing."

Esau said, "Isn't he rightly named Jacob? This is the second time he has taken advantage of me: He took my birthright, and now he's taken my blessing!" Then he asked, "Haven't you reserved any blessing for me?"

Isaac answered Esau, "I have made him lord over you and have made all his relatives his servants, and I have sustained him with grain and new wine. So what can I possibly do for you, my son?"

Esau said to his father, "Do you have only one blessing, my father? Bless me too, my father!" Then Esau wept aloud." (Genesis 27:30-38)

Rebekah lied. Jacob cheated. And the blessing, signed with Isaac's oath, could not be undone.

But cheaters never prosper, Rebekah and Jacob included. They didn't walk away without consequences. Furious, Esau planned his revenge. Once Isaac died, he would kill his little, lying brother. Rebekah heard the rumor and told Jacob to run far away to his Uncle Laban's house, to stay put and wait it out. And he did for 20 years! Rebekah died during that time, never kissed her favorite son before her last breath. And we learn this timeless truth: *Liars lose more.* We lie to get something, to keep something, not to lose something, but we end up losing so much more.

We end up losing so much more.

So what does this story mean for us today? I suppose we could talk about all the ways we are tempted to lie. With our parents. Our bosses. Our online image. And we could talk about all the ways those lies backfire and we lose out in the end. But I want to focus on two of the biggest lies that affect our souls, our churches, and our lives, two whoppers the father of lies, the devil, whispers to all of us all the time. Ready for them? Highlight these: Lie #1—You're too good. Lie #2—You're too bad.

You're too good. Have you ever heard of a book called *Selfie*? It's a fascinating look at how people in different generations have viewed themselves. The author tells the story of John Vasconcellos, a California politician who made self-esteem the new normal in American culture. John was raised with that ugly kind of religion that only told him he was rotten. It seems all he learned from his upbringing was that he was a sinner and always would be. But then John met a man who changed his mind. People weren't sinners, he was told. They were amazing. That thought transformed him, pushed him to embrace his feelings and shake off his old faith. Author Will Storr writes, "The problem, he decided, was that the people of America remained trapped under the old Christian delusion that humans were essentially rotten" (page 189). Vasconcellos was on a mission to bless every human being with self-esteem. Using his political power and new scientific research, he pushed and pushed and persuaded a momentous change in public views of self-esteem. By 1994, nearly 30 states approved over 170 statutes that promoted self-esteem in America, convinced by the research John often quoted. But guess what? It was a lie. Vasconcellos had ripped a quote from the research out of context, called something good that the data determined was not.

But the lie spread, and here we are in an age of self-esteem, self-help, and selfies. Spiritually you and I face a hundred lies connected to this one . . . you're too good. Do you need to pray about this? Nah, you're too good. Do you need to find truth outside of yourself, in Jesus' teaching, in God's Word? Nah, you're too good. Do you need a tough-loving spiritual community to question your motives, hold you accountable, call you to repentance? Nah, you're too good. Too good to believe God would want you to change. Too good to be in real spiritual danger. Too good to need to repent. Too good to go to hell. You're too good to need Jesus.

This is the lie that has replaced repentance, that has excommunicated the idea of excommunication. Author Will Storr, who is not a Christian, concludes, "It occurred to me that this might be the next irresistible step on the road we've taken: if we are all gods, then our feelings are sacred, and if our feelings are sacred, the people who hurt them must be sinners" (page 301). If you thought it was bad to pretend to be Esau, what about pretending to be God?

But there's another lie that's just as deceptive and even more destructive. *You're too bad.* Too bad to belong here. Too bad to confess what you've really done. Too bad to be real with people at church. Too bad to admit that. Too bad to be accepted by God. Too bad to be forgiven or saved or end up in heaven. Too bad to change. If you've ever feared being honest, ever wondered if God was done with you, ever thought even the cross of Jesus Christ wasn't enough to make God like you, accept you, adore you, then you've believed this lie—You're too bad. This is the lie that led Judas to hang himself. The lie that keeps people from coming to church. The lie that prevents so many from finding freedom in the good news of God's love.

So let me tell you the truth—We are bad, but God blesses bad people. Let me say it again—We've been bad, we've done bad, something in our hearts is still bad, but God blesses bad people. That's the truth!

Do you know why? Because of Jesus. Jesus came to save us from the sins of self-esteem, those narcissistic attempts to play God. Jesus came to save us from despair, the devastating thought that we are useless, rotten, unlovable. And that's exactly what Jesus did.

In fact, Jesus was so committed to that plan that he told the truth, even when it cost him. Even when people walked away, lost respect, picked up the nails, Jesus told the truth. He wouldn't flop like a forward looking for a penalty kick.

He is the Truth, and he told the truth for you.

No, he told the truth. "Are you the Christ?" they questioned Jesus at his trial. And one lie would have saved him. But he didn't lie so he could save you. "I am," he confessed. No deceit was found in Jesus' mouth. No dodging the question to save his own skin. He lived up to his nickname. He is the Truth, and he told the truth for you.

Back in 1925, golfer Bobby Jones told the truth. Jones, who later would cofound the Masters, was golfing in the U.S. Open when he had the chance to lie. As he prepared for a shot from the rough, his ball moved. No one saw it but Jones. But the truth was the truth. He called over an official and eventually lost the tournament. Reporters flocked to Jones, wondering why he did it. He told them not to make a big deal out of it. "You might as well praise me for not robbing banks," Jones said. But they did praise him. For nearly one hundred years people have praised him. A man who told the truth, even when it cost him.

Which is why we praise Jesus. Love him or hate him, crowd around him or crucify him, he would never lie. Do you know why? He didn't want to lose you. He wanted to be a sinless Savior, a perfect sacrifice. He wanted to die on a cross to change your name from liar to loved, from deceiver to daughter, from sinner to son, from Jacob to justified, from Rebekah to redeemed, from bad to blessed. Jesus, who is the Truth, changed us. No, you are not too good to need saving. And, no, you are not too bad to be saved. You need Jesus, and because of God's crazy love, you have him. That is the truth.

God's Truth for My Life

1. When are you most tempted to lie (blatant lie, exaggeration, withholding information, etc.)? Think about the reasons that lead you to lie. What do you want to get or keep so badly that you would give up your honesty?

2. Read 1 Peter 2:21–25. What good advice does Peter give us as he thinks about Jesus' behavior? What good news does he add as he thinks about Jesus' cross?

3. Evaluate: Being honest is one of the best ways to create genuine Christian community in a church.

Is God Here?

Mike Novotny

There's a single sentence that's changing my life. I know that sounds like an exaggeration, but I'm serious. One sentence is changing my life. In fact, the sentence has just three little words, only nine total letters. But I think about that sentence every day. Most mornings, after I yell at my alarm clock, that sentence is the first thing that pops into my mind. Most days that sentence helps me deal with situations I can't control. It rescues me from a mental spiral when I am criticized or the shame I feel when I sin. And, most important, that sentence is increasing my love for Jesus.

Before I reveal the sentence, I need to write about the power of presence. Not presents, like Christmas presents, but presence, being present, being here. Because there are few things more powerful than the right person's presence. What if I tell you, "_____ is here!"? You can fill in that blank with whomever you want. What if *that* person sits down right next to you and smiles? Whom would you pick? The guy you like from work? The girl you just started dating? Your new puppy? Your son who lives so far away? Your grandkids? Your best friend from way back? Your husband whom you lost? The baby you never got to meet? Ah, you feel that? That's the power of presence. When someone really good whom we really love is present, that presence is powerful. It changes us.

Which brings me back to my sentence. Those nine letters, those three words that are changing my life. Are you ready for them yet? Here goes—GOD is here! Oh, yes! GOD is here! I didn't write, "god is here." And I didn't write, "God is here." I wrote, "GOD is here!"

GOD is here. That sentence sounds simple, but it's not. To actually believe not in some boring god or in the theologically correct God, but in GOD, the invisible but bright and glorious and good and holy and worthy and majestic and thrilling and captivating and interesting GOD. And to believe GOD "is." Not GOD was here before you messed things up. Not GOD will be here one day when you go to heaven. I mean "is" right now. Present tense presence. GOD is "here." Not up there. Not over there. I mean right here. GOD is here! Do you believe that? Those three words can change you. If the presence of some person, some flawed, temporal, sinful person can change your emotions, what about the actual presence of GOD? What if I told you, "GOD is here!"?

GOD is here. That sentence sounds simple, but it's not.

I'm not the first person to be changed by that sentence. One of Jesus' dysfunctional family members was too. And maybe his story will change you too.

Let's continue our story about Jacob. Here's how this next chapter of his story begins: **"Jacob left Beersheba and set out for Harran"** (Genesis 28:10). Do you remember why Jacob is going from southern Israel up to modern-day Turkey? Because he is running. You see, Jacob has just impersonated his brother, lied to his blind father, and stolen the family blessing, a deception so vile his older brother is angry enough to kill him. So Jacob runs for his life to his uncle's house in Harran, 500-600 miles away.

"When he reached a certain place, he stopped for the night because the sun had set. Taking one of the stones there, he put it under his head and lay down to sleep" (Genesis 28:11). Jacob reaches a "certain place." That's a big deal in this story. A certain place. In other words, a place that is no place, not even worth mentioning. Later we learn the name of the place is Luz, but Luz is a two-camel town with zero Tripadvisor reviews. This is like Kloten, Wisconsin. Where? Exactly. (It's a suburb of Chilton, by the way . . . Where? Exactly.)

Which is where you live most of your life, right? Certain places. Nowhere special places. Your apartment in a hallway lined with apartments in an average apartment complex. Your locker squeezed in between hundreds of others, crammed with books and backpacks. Your cubicle, 25 square feet of Monday to Friday indentured service. Your 2000-whatever Toyota that hasn't been vacuumed since last year. Your nursing home that doesn't feel like home at all. Your driveway. Your jail cell. Your kids' school's parking lot. Your church's musty basement where the recovery group meets. These are not tourist stops. These are the "certain places" where we live.

But guess who shows up in "certain places"? **"[Jacob] had a dream in which he saw a stairway resting on the earth, with its top reaching to heaven, and the angels of God were ascending and descending on it. There above it stood the** LORD**"** (Genesis 28:12,13). Does Led Zeppelin pay royalties to the author of Genesis, the original stairway to heaven? What do stairways do? They let you reach a place you couldn't reach on your own. They let people get from here to there. This stairway connects heaven to earth, to this "certain place," to Jacob. And—look!—angels are going to and from that certain place, that nowhere place, angels! And—look!—the LORD! GOD is here! All capital letters LORD is a reference to the one and only true God, the glorious LORD, the great I AM, the God who exists everywhere, always keeping his promises to forgive and save. That GOD is here in this place? Yup.

And he has something to say:

And he said: "I am the Lᴏʀᴅ, the God of your father Abraham and the God of Isaac. I will give you and your descendants the land on which you are lying. Your descendants will be like the dust of the earth, and you will spread out to the west and to the east, to the north and to the south. All peoples on earth will be blessed through you and your offspring. I am with you and will watch over you wherever you go, and I will bring you back to this land. I will not leave you until I have done what I have promised you." (Genesis 28:13-15)

Five promises in three verses. I'll give your descendants this land, a promise fulfilled five hundred years later when Joshua marched into the Promised Land. Your family will be like the dust, a promise fulfilled in Egypt when Jacob's family grew so big even the pharaoh feared them. All peoples on earth will be blessed through your family, the Bible's biggest promise when Jesus, from Jacob's line, died for the sins of every race, tribe, nation, color, and people. I am with you right now, Jacob. And I will bring you home one day.

Five good promises given to one not-so-good guy. Remember what Jacob just did? Remember why he is running away from home? This teaches us so much about God. Recently, I met a woman who grew up with an angry God. She went to church, but church was more about guilt, about fear, about strict rules and not good news. I thought of her when I read these words. This GOD is not her childhood god. They sound the same, but the god of guilt is a lowercase, man-made character of fiction. GOD, the true GOD, is this GOD, Jacob's GOD, a GOD who takes sin seriously but who loves to forgive and make good promises to people who have been bad. He is a GOD who doesn't let sin push him away over there, but a GOD who comes right here.

And Jacob gets it:

> **When Jacob awoke from his sleep, he thought, "Surely the LORD is in this place, and I was not aware of it." He was afraid and said, "How awesome is this place! This is none other than the house of God; this is the gate of heaven."** (Genesis 28:16,17)

"This place! I thought this was no place. Just a certain place. Just another place. But the LORD is in this place! I didn't see it. I didn't get it. But now I know—How awesome is this place! This is the house of God. This is where God lives. GOD is here!"

Jacob doesn't want to forget the glorious place where he learned that glorious truth.

> **Early the next morning Jacob took the stone he had placed under his head and set it up as a pillar and poured oil on top of it. He called that place Bethel, though the city used to be called Luz. Then Jacob made a vow, saying, "If God will be with me and will watch over me on this journey I am taking and will give me food to eat and clothes to wear so that I return safely to my father's household, then the LORD will be my God and this stone that I have set up as a pillar will be God's house, and of all that you give me I will give you a tenth."** (Genesis 28:18–22)

Jacob, who would later have his name changed, changed the name of that place. "Luz? No, let's call it Bethel (Hebrew for 'house of God'). This is not just any place. This is *the* place. This is the place where GOD is."

In 2007 the *Washington Post* conducted a social experiment by placing greatness in a "certain place," a D.C. metro platform where the homeless often beg for change. Violin virtuoso Joshua Bell grabbed his $3.5 million violin and played a free concert for 45 minutes, filling the station with the same sounds that cost concertgoers $100 a ticket just three days earlier. In those 45 minutes, 1,070 people heard

That is the key to spiritual happiness, to peace, to joy, to contentment.

Bell's music. Do you know how much they dropped in his empty violin case? $32! Do you know how many stopped for even a second to listen? 7! And do you know how many people recognized one of the world's greatest musicians? Just one. One shocked woman stopped her morning rush, listened, and gasped to be in the presence of someone truly great.

God wants you to be that woman. The one who stops. The one who listens. The one who wakes up from the rush of this restless world to gasp, "GOD is here! I didn't know it then, but GOD is here!" That is the sentence, the truth, the faith that will change you. That is the key to spiritual happiness, to peace, to joy, to contentment. GOD is here. So how do you do that? Let me give you three tips—First, believe in *GOD*. Second, believe in *is*. Third, believe in *here*.

First, believe in *GOD*—a big, beautiful, glorious GOD. To be honest, I missed this growing up. I got the whole Jesus thing, the forgiveness of my sins, the gift of heaven, and I'm so glad I did. I got grace, but I didn't get GOD. I didn't get that GOD is a big deal. I wanted to get to heaven to get out of my pain; I didn't think about getting into his presence. But now I get it—GOD! GOD is the reason Jesus came, the reason we have forgiveness, the reason why heaven is heaven. A GOD who is better than anything and anyone on earth. More glorious than the Grand Canyon. More beautiful than my baby girls. More interesting than the best book. More relaxing than my favorite couch. More breathtaking than a sunset. More thrilling than good sex. More satisfying than a loaf of fresh bread and a plate of olive oil. GOD is better than anything I have ever experienced!

My friend Katie and I talked about this the other day. I asked her, "Who would be the most amazing, thrilling, exciting, life-changing person to walk through that door and be right here with us?"

Katie leaned in and muttered, "I'm supposed to say Jesus, right? Because I'm thinking about someone delivering food. Sushi! Yes! A guy with sushi! . . . but I love dolphins too. Can a dolphin show up?"

"You bet," I said. "How about a dolphin swims through that door with a rainbow roll on its dorsal fin?" And Katie got so, so happy. I did too. Because it's easy to forget GOD is GOD. Jesus is even better than that. Every day we have to remind our hearts of that fact. This, this, this is not anywhere close to as good as GOD. That is why every good thing in life is GOD's way of showing us he is not some god. He's GOD.

Second, believe GOD *is*, not was, not will be. GOD is here. Remember what Jesus said, "Surely I am with you always. I am. Not I will be." This is what eternal life is in the Bible: to be with God forever, starting now. Not a future promise but a present gift. King David once taught, **"I will fear no evil, for you are with me"** (Psalm 23:4). If you believe in Jesus, trust in his forgiveness for your sins; GOD is with you. Already. You're not in the waiting room. You don't have to be afraid of death or cancer or credit card bills or what those people might think about you or your performance or your reputation because no matter what, GOD is here.

Third, believe GOD is *here*. Right here. In this certain place. In your Toyota, your nursing home room, your average church. GOD is here. The devil doesn't want you to believe that. He says, "You are far from him after what you did. The best you can pray is, 'God, are you up there . . . maybe?'" No, no, no. GOD is here. You have a stairway to heaven right here. Actually, that's my favorite part. Two thousand years after Jacob's dream, Jesus showed up. And when a guy named Philip found him, he ran to his friend and said, "Nathanael, he's here! The Messiah is here! He's from Nazareth!" Know what Nathanael said, "Nazareth? Yeah right" (see John 1:43–51). But then Jesus showed up and said this, **"Very truly I tell you, you will see 'heaven open, and the angels of God ascending and descending on' the Son of Man"** (John 1:51). Did you catch it? What were the angels ascending and descending on in Genesis chapter 28 in Jacob's dream? The stairway. And what was the stairway? The connection between God and man. But what does Jesus say here in John chapter 1? "You'll see the angels ascending and descending on me, the Son of Man. I am the stairway. I am the stairway to heaven. I am the way you and GOD get connected. Because of me, my life, my death, my blood, my resurrection, GOD is right here in this place with you."

Oh! GOD is here! That changed me. I wake up, and I don't know how the day will go. I don't know who will be here. But instead of living in fear of what might be, I say, "In your presence, God, there is fullness of joy. I will fear no evil, for you are with me. GOD is here!"

There was once a blind man who didn't see his wife until the day of their wedding. William Dyke had been blinded in an accident years earlier, but that didn't stop him from dating and proposing to an incredible woman. But he never saw her until a surgeon said he could help. William agreed, the surgery happened, the bandages were scheduled to be removed on the day of his wedding. In front of the church, they met and he saw her. But in his mind he had already seen enough to love her, to treasure her presence. Our bandages won't come off until heaven, but we have already "seen" Jesus enough to love him, to treasure his presence, to love that simple sentence—GOD is here!

God's Truth for My Life

1. Do you believe in god, God, or GOD? In other words, is GOD the most exciting, thrilling, interesting, comforting, and loving person you have ever met? If so, how did you come to believe that? If not, who tops him on your list?

2. Read Philippians 4:4-13, one of the Bible's most inspiring sections about joy, peace, and contentment. Where do you see the power of God's present presence?

3. Read Psalm 16 and find at least four connections to the message in this chapter.

How Does Grace Change Me?

Mike Novotny

In the Sistine Chapel, on the massive painting behind the main altar, on the very bottom right corner is a picture of . . . karma. Payback. Revenge. At first glance, it might look like just another odd scene in Michelangelo's famous fresco of the last judgment. A muscular man with long, pointy donkey ears, standing in the darkness of hell, wrapped in a massive snake who is (sorry for this detail) biting his private parts. Kind of weird. But what you may not know is that the man was an actual person Michelangelo knew. His name was Biagio da Cesena. Biagio, who worked for the pope at that time, had dared to criticize Michelangelo's work, claiming nude paintings had no place in a place of Christian worship. In response, the offended Michelangelo painted Biagio's face into his painting right on the hell-bound, donkey-eared, serpent-wrapped man who is currently seen by six million people each year. Ah, payback.

I tell you that because karma is a sin that tempts all of us at home, at school, at work, on the field, in the church. Nothing is more natural (no YouTube tutorial required), logical (so easy to justify), and dangerous to happy marriages, stable families, or drama-free lives than karma. He does this, so she does that; then he says this, and she says that and . . . karma.

Two people vow to love each other for better or worse. But then he leaves his stuff for her to clean up, so she complains about not being his mother, so he brings up some totally unrelated flaw of hers, so she gets defensive and lists all the things she does at home, so they don't make love, so he escapes to work, so she . . . you get it. Karma. She Snapchats this, so she snaps back, so she private messages them about her while she says mean things about . . . You've seen it. Karma. A pitcher hits their batter, so their pitcher hits their batter. So they rush the mound and brawl. Karma. Christian A at church gossips, so Christian B gossips back. She gets passive-aggressive, so she holds a grudge, so they both think about each other instead of God at church. Karma. Karma is a crazy cycle that doesn't end. Karma kills us.

Why we do it? Why don't fighting families and dysfunctional churches and bitter rivals just put down their fists, say sorry, and agree to no more karma and no more drama? Psychologists would suggest because of the fundamental attribution error. Ever heard of it? It's a theory that says we humans have an internal bias where we believe those people do bad things because they are bad people, but we do bad things because of bad circumstances (which means we weren't really doing bad things). In other words, it's their fault, not mine.

Karma is a crazy cycle that doesn't end. Karma kills us.

I once heard of a pastor who experienced this in a vivid way. When couples were on the verge of divorce, he would say to one, "Draw me a pie chart that divides up the blame. What's your fault? What's his?" Of course, it was never 50/50. It was always a majority the other spouse's fault. But the pastor wouldn't argue that. Instead, he'd say, "Okay, let's just talk today about this little slice that's your fault. Let's find a time to apologize for that. Let's pray for God to change that about you." But do you know what the pastor found? No one would do it. No one. They couldn't even own their little slice. They'd excuse it because of something he did or she said. They attributed the error to the other person. And the craziness of karma continued. Without God's intervention, it will for you too. Karma will spiral and slowly kill you.

Which is why I need to tell you a true story about the karma in Jesus' family tree. It's a long, exhausting story about a family that refused to own their part, refused to confess their sins, refused to forgive. This story is God's way of warning us about continuing the karma. At the same time, it's a reminder that only grace, only undeserved love, can save us.

Let's go back to Jacob, the grandson of Abraham, the dude who has just lied to his blind father to steal a blessing from his big brother. That Jacob just ran from home to save his neck and finally arrives at his Uncle Laban's home. And the ugly story starts beautifully:

> **After Jacob had stayed with him for a whole month, Laban said to him, "Just because you are a relative of mine, should you work for me for nothing? Tell me what your wages should be."**
>
> **Now Laban had two daughters; the name of the older was Leah, and the name of the younger was Rachel. Leah had weak eyes, but Rachel had a lovely figure and was beautiful. Jacob was in love with Rachel and said, "I'll work for you seven years in return for your younger daughter Rachel."**
>
> **Laban said, "It's better that I give her to you than to some other man. Stay here with me." So Jacob served seven years to get Rachel, but they seemed like only a few days to him because of his love for her. (Genesis 29:14-20)**

And all the romantics say, "Awww!" Jacob falls for Laban's cover-girl daughter, Rachel. She's described as "beautiful" with "a lovely figure." With beautiful Rachel on his mind, seven years of sheepherding fly by.

But what Jacob doesn't know is that his Uncle Laban has the same smart, selfish, and deceptive brain as Jacob himself and the mother who raised him. He doesn't know Laban is about to start 13 years of drama.

> **Then Jacob said to Laban, "Give me my wife. My time is completed, and I want to make love to her."**
>
> **So Laban brought together all the people of the place and gave a feast. But when evening came, he took his daughter Leah and brought her to Jacob, and Jacob made love to her. And Laban gave his servant Zilpah to his daughter as her attendant.**
>
> **When morning came, there was Leah! So Jacob said to Laban, "What is this you have done to me? I served you for Rachel, didn't I? Why have you deceived me?"**
>
> **Laban replied, "It is not our custom here to give the younger daughter in marriage before the older one. Finish this daughter's bridal week; then we will give you the younger one also, in return for another seven years of work."** (Genesis 29:21–27)

That's messed up! The ol' sister swap. How in the world did that happen? Was it pitch-black in the pre-electricity tent? Was Jacob that drunk? Was Leah wearing a thick veil? We don't know, but we do know karma caught up to Jacob.

Does this sound familiar—a lying parent uses their own kid to deceive a man who can't see to get something they want? That's what Jacob did to his dad. That's what his uncle did to him.

The drama is nowhere near over. Jacob marries both Leah and Rachel, starting the first season of *Sister Wives*. And the first episode is called "Baby Momma Karma Drama." Leah is not loved, but she's a baby-making machine. Rachel is a cover girl, but she can't have kids. This family implodes. Leah has a son, Reuben, which means "God has seen my misery!" And another, Simeon, which means "'God heard' that I'm not loved." Then Levi, which means "my husband will finally be 'attached' to me." Then Judah.

Then Rachel gets jealous and gives her servant girl Bilhah to Jacob. Bilhah gets pregnant and has a son, Dan, which means "God has 'vindicated' me." Then Naphtali, which means "I've won a 'struggle' with my sister."

Then Leah gives her servant girl Zilpah to Jacob, and she has a son, Gad, which means "good fortune," and another, Asher, which means "how 'happy' I am." And then it gets really messed up. Leah's firstborn brings home some mandrakes, a plant Rachel believes will help her have a baby (because its roots look like a little person), and Rachel wants a baby, so she trades her bedtime sex appointment to her sister for some mandrakes, and Leah shows up and tells her husband, "I've hired you. You have to sleep with me!" (I'm not making this up, people!) He does, and she has another son, Issachar, which means "God has 'rewarded' me" and then another, Zebulun, which means "my husband will finally 'honor' me." Then finally, Rachel has her own son. And guess what she names him? Joseph, which is Hebrew for "may God give me another!"

But the family drama is still not over. God tells Jacob it's time to go home, so he bolts without telling Laban. Jacob packs up his wives, his kids, his flocks and runs. Rachel even steals Laban's household gods, stuffing them in her camel's saddlebags before they take off. Laban, furious, chases Jacob down and, after seven days, catches him. And the two bitter men blow up!

"Why did you lie to me? Why did you steal my gods?"

"Steal? I didn't steal a thing, you liar. Check!"

So Laban rummages through every tent and only has the saddlebags on the camels left to check. But Rachel lies, "Daddy, I'm sorry. I can't get up. I'm having my period."

Laban's not touching that, so he instead explodes on Jacob, and Jacob explodes right back. They accuse each other. They shove fingers in each other's faces. They draw their pie charts with 100% blame on the other guy. And, when no one budges, they make a deal. They set up a pillar and say, "If you cross this line, may God come after you. And if you cross this line, may God punish you." And with that, Laban goes home. The end.

Wow. 3 entire chapters. 133 verses. 20 total years. And why is this all in the Bible? Why did God want his people to read this story for all of history? To prove this point: Karma is long-term drama. If you want to go years with maximum drama, then give people what you think they deserve. Choose karma.

Do you know what a Newton's Cradle is? I think my dad had one of them on his desk back in the day. It has five metal spheres that show how force is pushed through the middle spheres. When you pull back on the first one, you send the fifth one flying. This is like karma. You might smack someone, and they might smack you back, and then it's even, right? Not a chance. What actually happens? You sin. They sin. You sin. They sin. You sin. They sin. You say. She says.

You do. She does. You text. She texts. And people get caught in the middle—kids, mutual friends, coworkers, parents. But, unlike Newton's Cradle, the traumatic force doesn't diminish. It grows.

So where are you settling for karma? With whom are you not being loving or patient or humble or gentle or kind or forgiving or generous but attributing the drama to their sins? Whose chunk of the blame pie are you focusing on instead of owning your own slice? Yes, I'm sure what they did was wrong. I hope they repent and own their slice. And there are some abusive

Whose chunk of the blame pie are you focusing on?

situations that some of you should leave alone. But Jacob's story is God's warning. Don't play that game. Don't believe the lie that this is going to end. Don't waste the next 20 years trying to settle the score. You won't. You can't. The Chinese proverb is right: He who seeks revenge should dig two graves. So do the unnatural, the illogical.

Instead, choose the way of Jesus: **"If anyone slaps you on the right cheek, turn to them the other cheek also. . . . I tell you, love your enemies and pray for those who persecute you"** (Matthew 5:39,44). Like his friend Peter wrote, **"Do not repay evil with evil or insult with insult. On the contrary, repay evil with blessing, because to this you were called so that you may inherit a blessing"** (1 Peter 3:9). God wants to bless you with less drama, with more forgiveness.

Why? Because God isn't into karma. He's not into treating people as their sins deserve. He's into blessing bad people in surprising ways. Did you see that in this story, in the "Baby Momma Karma Drama"? Did you notice what God was up to? Keeping his promise. He promised a massive family to Abraham, Isaac, and Jacob, and, finally, here it comes. All those sons would become the 12 tribes of Israel. And guess who would one day show up from the tribe of Judah? Jesus, the Son of God, who is full of grace and truth.

Instead of giving it back to sinners like us, what did Jesus do? He loved. He forgave. He saved. As he was hanging on a cross, Jesus prayed, "Father, forgive them. Father, don't remember their sins. Father, don't keep score. Instead, save." And he did. Through Jesus, we have grace on top of grace.

Through Jesus, we have grace on top of grace.

We have a God who does not treat us as our sins deserve. We have a God who gave us a cross instead of karma. We have a God who keeps blessing us despite our sins, a God who loves us without strings attached, a God who changes our names from sinners to saints. Because of grace, there is no drama with God, no payback, no revenge. Just love and acceptance and his presence with us. Grace saved us from all those fears. Grace gave us the blessings of God. Karma kills but grace saves.

Because of God's grace, we are God's chosen people and we lay claim to the blessings given to Jacob. The meaning behind his children's names is true for us. Like Reuben, God sees our misery and drama. Like Simeon, he hears us when we pray. Like Levi, God is attached to us. Like Judah, we praise the God of grace. Like Dan, we are vindicated, cleared of blame for our sins. Like Naphtali, we have won a great struggle against the enemy. Like Gad and Asher, we have good fortune and are happy because of God's love. Like Issachar, Jesus is our reward. Like Zebulun, God honors us with a seat at his table. And like Joseph, God adds even more. Blessing after blessing. Grace on top of grace. We are holy men and women, because grace saves.

Karma will kill us, but grace can save us. It already has.

God's Truth for My Life

1. In which of your current relationships are you living by karma instead of by grace? What would it look like to own your sins in that relationship? What would it look like to show that person grace?

2. Agree/Disagree: Scores rarely get settled because sinners keep scores in selfish ways.

3. Study Romans 5:8 and contrast God's love with the idea of karma.

How Boldly Can I Pray?

Mike Novotny

There are few things as important in our lives as trust, as knowing the people in our lives are faithful, reliable, and trustworthy. Just like what happens when you're dating someone you don't really trust compared to someone you do. Or when you're married to someone you trust to listen to you, to try to understand you, to try to serve your family. Couples can get through almost anything

Trust makes honesty possible.

with trust. Or think about the people you go to school with or work with or your roommates or the people at your Bible study. A lack of trust keeps us guarded, anxious, and afraid, but trust makes honesty possible. It makes it possible to confess to each other, be real with each other, and to really help each other. So much of life comes down to this one thing—trust. This is important: *You can get through anything with trust.*

And that is so true with God. So much of this hope and peace and confidence we talk about as Christians comes down to trusting God, to believing he is who he says he is, having faith that God is faithful. You can get through struggles and sin and death itself if you trust. In fact, there are people right now who are going through the same stuff as you, but they've found more peace of mind, more confidence, more happiness because of trust. Which is why I want to give you a trust booster.

It's another weird story from the Bible about our friend Jacob, the guy who is rather famous for not being trustworthy. Yet in this story, Jacob gives us a vivid example of how to trust in God when you're facing your biggest fears.

Let me take you back to one of the most terrifying nights of Jacob's life. He's about to be reunited with his twin brother, Esau, after 20 years apart. But Jacob is afraid. You see, the last time the twins saw each other, Jacob was dressed up in Esau's clothes, impersonating his brother to lie to his blind father to steal Esau's blessing, Esau's right to run their family. Esau was angry enough to kill him, so Jacob ran and crashed with his uncle for two decades. But now, finally, Jacob is heading home with his 4 lady friends and his 11 sons. That's when he hears Esau is marching out to meet him . . . with four hundred men.

"That night Jacob got up and took his two wives, his two female servants and his eleven sons and crossed the ford of the Jabbok. After he had sent them across the stream, he sent over all his possessions. So Jacob was left alone" (Genesis 32:22–24). It's just Jacob there at the Jabbok, just east of the Jordan River, about halfway between the Sea of Galilee and the Dead Sea. He has a lot to think about because he and his 11 sons might die the next day. They can't fight off hairy Esau and his band of angry men.

But while Jacob is thinking about all this, one of the weirdest things in the entire Bible happens: **"So Jacob was left alone, and a man wrestled with him till daybreak"** (verse 24). What? Some dude just shows up and jumps off the top turnbuckle! Some rando puts 97-year-old Jacob in a figure-four leg lock, and they wrestle for hours, the Bible says, until daybreak. Ever wrestled your brother before? After a few minutes, you're sweating and panting and your muscles are burning and your hair is nasty. And elderly Jacob wrestles this guy in the dust for hours!

"When the man saw that he could not overpower him,

he touched the socket of Jacob's hip so that his hip was wrenched as he wrestled with the man" (verse 25). Jacob isn't going to roll over and get pinned. He's scrappy for a guy who's about to get into the Smucker's Club. But then the man touches his hip and—pop!—snaps it right out of the socket. (I YouTubed dislocated hip videos, and they are not pleasant.) But wait . . . what man could dislocate your hip with the touch of his hand? This has to be more than just a man. This has to be . . . God? Jacob, in the midst of twisting out of a reverse arm bar, realizes he is wrestling with God!

Then comes the key verse: **"Then the man said, 'Let me go, for it is daybreak.' But Jacob replied, 'I will not let you go unless you bless me'"** (verse 26). God must have had a 7:00 A.M. appointment because he needs to go, but Jacob won't let him. His fingers clamp on to his arms. With a dislocated hip, Jacob can't be grappling with him. He has to be holding on to him, desperately clinging to his ankle while God tries to get away. But look what Jacob says. (This is huge!) "I won't let you go unless you bless me. You're not leaving until you bless me. Don't you even think about walking away until you do something good for me."

This is what I don't want you to miss. Way back in Genesis chapter 28, when Jacob dreamed of a stairway to heaven, God said Jacob's family would be like the dust of the earth. Then in Genesis chapter 32, just before this guy showed up, Jacob said, **"Save me, I pray, from the hand of my brother Esau, for I am afraid he will come and attack me, and also the mothers with their children. But you have said, 'I will surely make you prosper and will make your descendants like the sand of the sea, which cannot be counted'"** (verses 11,12). "But you have said. You said, God, I would become a great nation, but I'm not yet. You said, God, my family would be like the sand of the sea, but we're not yet. I'm afraid I'm going to die, God, but you said." What is Jacob doing? He's clinging to what God said. His heart is doing to God's Word what his arms are doing to his opponent. He's holding on. He's trusting God is faithful. He's trusting God is not a liar. He's trusting God has to do what he said. "But, God," Jacob is pleading, "you said!"

Parents, have you ever gotten busted by those two words—*you said*? A few weeks back, I was making plans with the kids for our family day. I promised, "We're going to eat lunch and take naps and do the Slip and Slide and make dinner and read the Bible and watch a movie and play some board games." But, as I should have guessed, we couldn't fit in everything that I planned. But when I told them we ran out of time for games, that they couldn't stay up until ten, that it was time to brush their teeth, want to guess what they said? "But, Dad! You . . . said!" (Kids, listen up. Your parents are liars. We don't mean to lie, but we do. We are unintentional liars. We forget we are not God. We run out of time and energy and money. Plans change.)

But this is the amazing part about our Father in *heaven*. He's a capital-*F* Father. He's not just another father here on earth. He's GOD. He is all-knowing, so nothing surprises him and messes with his plans. He is all-powerful, so he never runs out of energy, never needs a nap, never says, "I'd love to, kid, but Daddy is too tired." He's GOD! And, most important, GOD is holy. That means he can't sin. He can't lie, even unintentionally. He's faithful. Highlight this: *Trusting prayers start, "But you said!"* GOD has to do what he says. He has to. You can say to God, "You have to, God. You said!"

Have you ever prayed like that? Like Jacob, have you ever clung to God desperately and insisted that he do what he said he would do? Because that is where peace is found. This is how you get rid of fear. This is how you deal with guilt. You grab hold of God and you demand, "But you said!" Let me give you three examples.

First, think of your pain, the hard stuff in your life. Jesus says you can pray, "But you said you'd do good!" In Romans 8:28, he said, **"And we know that in all things God works for the good of those who love him, who have been called according to his purpose."** So you can pray, "God, the results aren't good. Cancer. MS. Bipolar disorder. And I can't see how this could be good. But you said you would never let something like this happen to someone who loves you without using it for good. So do something good, God. Let me meet someone at chemo or at my support group who doesn't know you. Cure me so my cousin starts to believe again. Strip me of my idols so I realize all I need is you. Bring someone to faith at my funeral, but do something good, God. You have to. You said."

> **"Do something good, God. You have to. You said."**

Or, second, think about prayer. Jesus says you can pray, "But you said prayer works!" In James 5:16, he said, **"The prayer of a righteous person is powerful and effective."** So you pray, "God, you made me righteous. You sent Jesus to make me right with you. And you said when people like me pray, it's powerful. When I pray for my kids who are too busy for church . . . When I pray for a job so I can pay these bills . . . When I pray for you to take me home because I'm tired, it's powerful. But I don't see it, God. I tried and nothing happened. I prayed and nothing changed. But you said, God. Powerful. Effective. So do something. This can't be pointless, God. Because you said."

Or think about forgiveness. Jesus says you can pray, "But you said you'd forgive everything." In 1 John 1:9, he said, **"If we confess our sins, [God] is faithful and just and will for-**

give us our sins and purify us from all unrighteousness."
So you pray, "God, you said you will forgive us, not you might forgive us. You will. And you said all. Not some of my sins. Not the normal ones. All my unrighteousness. My relapse. My lack of passion for you. My constant complaining about my First World life. You said you'd forgive it all. That's hard for me to believe, God. Hard to think you would forgive me again, that I am purified in your eyes, that you're not thinking about what's wrong with me, that you see me as righteous, that I'm all right. I wouldn't do that for me, God, but you said. You said."

Oh, what a way to pray! And you can do it with any promise. "God, you said your Word would never come back empty, and I shared your Word with my brother. God, you said those who believe in you would live, even if they die, and my mom believed in you. God, you said you'd be with me, even if I feel alone, and that's how I feel. God, you said!"

He loves it when you hold on to him.

You might think that's offensive to God, but it's not. He loves it when you hold on to him like Jacob because it shows you trust him. You believe God's not a liar. He's faithful. The reformer Martin Luther once wrote, "Prayer is not overcoming God's reluctance but laying hold of his willingness." It's laying hold of God's will to bless you. God's will is to bless you. God wants to bless you.

Why? Why would God give us the right to talk to him like that? The answer to that question is how Jacob's wrestling match ends:

The man asked him, "What is your name?"

"Jacob," he answered.

Then the man said, "Your name will no longer be Jacob, but Israel, because you have struggled with God and with humans and have overcome."

Jacob said, "Please tell me your name."

But he replied, "Why do you ask my name?" Then he blessed him there.

So Jacob called the place Peniel, saying, "It is because I saw God face to face, and yet my life was spared."

The sun rose above him as he passed Peniel, and he was limping because of his hip. (Genesis 32:27–31)

Why can we talk to God so boldly? Because our God is a name changer. God changed Jacob's name, which means "heel grabber/deceiver/liar," into Israel, which means "struggles with God/wrestles with God/clings to God." And because of his name, Jacob could see God's face and live, not run from the frown of God but believe God's face was shining on him, being gracious to him, wanting to bless him.

And, Christian, that is true for you too. You might be limping because of life, but you can trust the God who has changed your name. God calls Christians 682 different names in the New Testament. Some are honest about our sinfulness. We are called weak, of little faith, sinners. But most, almost all, are reminders that Jesus' love and life and death and resurrection changed our names. In fact, out of the 682 names in the New Testament, 612 are positive! God says we are saved and perfect and righteous and redeemed and his people and his treasure and his nation and his kingdom, all through faith in Jesus.

You might be wrestling with those names. You might think, "Holy? Not me. You don't know what I've done. You don't know what I've thought. You don't know what I've said." True, but I know what God said. And God said the blood of Jesus works. The grace of God is enough. The love of God is for all. And because of Jesus, you get a new name.

Which is why you can say, "You said." You are a friend of God, a son of the King, the bride of Christ. He listens when you pray. He's not offended by your boldness. He'll be honored that you trusted him. Highlight this last thing: *We trust the God who changed our names.*

God's Truth for My Life

1. Consider your current practice of prayer. How could this chapter's message encourage you to talk more regularly and boldly with your Father in heaven?

2. Did my research about the "names" for Christians in the New Testament surprise you? Why or why not? How could they affect your prayer life?

3. Challenge: Spend three minutes praying one of the three "trusting prayers" mentioned in the message, including situations from your personal life. Hold God to his promises!

Flaw Upon Flaw

Bruce Becker

There's an old proverb that says, the apple never falls far from the tree. It's similar in meaning to other proverbs or adages like a chip off the old block; like father, like son; or like mother, like daughter. The apple adage simply means that children often reflect their parents and do so in a variety of ways. It could be physical, emotional, or relational qualities. It could be giftedness in the professional trades, in music, sports, or the arts. It could also be personality quirks or negative qualities such as anger issues or personal addictions. There is plenty of intrinsic evidence that the apple never falls far from the tree.

As I mentioned in the introduction of this book, Jacob could very well be the poster child for "flawed, but blessed." And if the apple adage holds true, then Jacob's flaws and his blessings could be a reflection of his parents' flaws and blessings. Could Jacob's flaws and blessings also be reflected in his own children's lives? I think we can expect it.

Let's dig deeper into the life of Jacob and check out whether or not apples fall far from the tree. We want to consider two of Jacob's bigger and more destructive flaws.

Deception 1.0

In "Why Does God Love Me?" Pastor Mike introduced us to the twin boys born to Isaac and Rebekah, namely Esau and Jacob. As Pastor Mike explained, Esau's name seems to mean "doer," and Jacob's name means a "heel grabber."

The term *heel grabber* is also a Hebrew idiom for "to take advantage of," "to trip up," or "to deceive." With Jacob's theft of Esau's birthright for a bowl of soup, he "earned" the title of "deceiver."

In "Why Does God Love Liars?" Pastor Mike shared the story of Jacob's second deception. Jacob teamed up with his mother, Rebekah, to trick Isaac into giving Jacob the birthright blessing, one that Isaac had planned to give to Esau.

Pastor Mike left off the story with Jacob running away to his Uncle Laban's house because his brother wanted to kill him, but there's a little more to the story that you might find interesting . . .

Rebekah was told (perhaps by a servant?) about Esau's plan to kill Jacob, so she encouraged Jacob to leave for a little while until his brother's anger subsided. But it appears that Rebekah didn't share Esau's revenge plan with Isaac. Instead, she said to Isaac: **"I'm disgusted with living because of these Hittite women. If Jacob takes a wife from among the women of this land, from Hittite women like these, my life will not be worth living"** (Genesis 27:46). Rebekah was referring to two Hittite women whom Esau married when he was 40 years old. These two women caused great heartache for Isaac and Rebekah.

As a result of Rebekah's disgust,

> **Isaac called for Jacob and blessed him. Then he commanded him: "Do not marry a Canaanite woman. Go at once to Paddan Aram, to the house of your mother's father Bethuel. Take a wife for yourself there, from among the daughters of Laban, your mother's brother."** (Genesis 28:1,2)

Before Jacob left, Isaac gave him a blessing, likely the

blessing that Isaac had planned to give Jacob all along:

> **"May God Almighty bless you and make you fruitful and increase your numbers until you become a community of peoples. May he give you and your descendants the blessing given to Abraham, so that you may take possession of the land where you now reside as a foreigner, the land God gave to Abraham."** (Genesis 28:3,4)

Jacob obeyed his father's command and headed north about 500-600 miles to Paddan Aram, also known as Harran. This is where Jacob's grandfather Abraham had lived for a time with his father, Terah.

When Rebekah urged Jacob to live with her brother, Laban, for "awhile," she anticipated that he would return sooner rather than later. The "awhile," however, lasted 20 years, and she would never see her favored son again.

Before we close this first chapter of Jacob's life, perhaps it is a good time to assess what we've learned about Jacob and about ourselves.

Jacob took advantage of his brother and deceived both his brother and his father. He did it in order to take control of his own life instead of relying on the promises of God. He was like his mother, Rebekah. She was willing to deceive her own husband in order to get what she wanted. It seems that in the case of Rebekah and Jacob, the apple didn't fall far from the tree.

Esau was not a God-fearing man. He didn't value the important things in life, like a relationship with the Lord—the God of free and faithful grace. He despised his birthright, willing to sell it for a bowl of soup. He was consumed with hate because of what his brother did to him and was prepared to get revenge.

Both Isaac and Rebekah displayed a lack of trust in the promises of God. They took matters into their own hands. They conspired to do what they wanted to do, even if it meant disobeying God and disrespecting each other.

Flaw upon flaw.

God's Truth for My Life

1. As you were growing up, what flaws or unhealthy tendencies did you observe in your parents?

2. As an adult, which of those flaws do you see when you look in the mirror?

3. If you have children or grandchildren, do you see any of those tendencies in their lives?

4. Being the target of deception can be a cruel and painful experience. Share an experience of deception, either a personal one or one from the life of someone you know. How does a person get passed having been deceived?

5. Have you ever been impatient with God and taken matters into your own hands? Give an example from your life.

6. Esau is an example of a person who placed personal needs and desires above his spiritual relationship with God. What warning does Esau's attitude have for you?

7. After Jacob deceived his father and angered his brother, he fled to Uncle Laban's. He left with nothing but the clothes on his back. What lesson does Jacob teach you about the consequences of deception?

Deception 2.0

Looking ahead to Jacob's second major flaw—showing favoritism—it appears that when it came to favoritism, the apple again didn't fall far from the tree. Both Isaac and Rebekah were guilty of this common parental flaw of showing favoritism to their kids. **"Isaac, who had a taste for wild game, loved Esau, but Rebekah loved Jacob"** (Genesis 25:28). And, in the not too distant future, Jacob would repeat his parents' mistake.

The stories of families portrayed in the Bible are often brutally honest. There is often no masking of what went on. These are the kinds of stories that most families would want

Showing favoritism destroys individuals and families.

to keep private, but God has included them in his Word to teach us and to warn us. Simply put, showing favoritism destroys individuals and families. King Solomon said it quite succinctly when he wrote, **"To show partiality is not good"** (Proverbs 28:21).

With Jacob leaving his home in Beersheba, the Lord initiated a personal training program for Jacob—not a physical one, but a spiritual one. Through a series of events in his life plus multiple encounters directly with God, Jacob would return home 20 years later a changed man. He left as Jacob, the heel grabber. He would return as Israel, the man who struggled with God and overcame. But we'll have to wait until later to witness the blessing upon blessing for Jacob.

It probably took Jacob three to four weeks to travel the 500-600 miles from Beersheba to Harran. As he approached his destination, he came upon a well that was not far from Laban's home. He saw three flocks of sheep lying near the well, but no one was watering their sheep. There was also a big stone covering the opening to the well.

Jacob struck up a conversation with those at the well, asking if anyone knew Laban. They did because they were also from Harran. In fact, one of the shepherds pointed out to Jacob that Laban's daughter Rachel was bringing her flock to the well. Rachel was a shepherdess. When Rachel arrived, Jacob's reaction was quite emotional. He went and moved the stone from the well so he could water Laban's sheep for Rachel. He then kissed her and began to weep aloud. Rachel, in turn, went to tell her father that Jacob was at the well. When Laban heard that his nephew had arrived, **"he hurried to meet him. He embraced him and kissed him and brought him to his home, and there Jacob told him all these things. Then Laban said to him, 'You are my own flesh and blood'"** (Genesis 29:13,14).

This comment of Laban's seems innocent enough. He may have been referring to their blood relationship. But could there have been more to it? Jacob had just told Laban why he was coming for a visit. Jacob and his mother, Rebekah, had deceived Isaac into giving him the blessing and Jacob's brother, Esau, was planning to kill him. Could Laban have also been saying, "The apple doesn't fall very far from the family tree?" Perhaps. Jacob was about to find out how deceptive and manipulative his mother's brother, Laban, could be.

In "How Does Grace Change Me?" Pastor Mike told the story of how Laban deceived Jacob. This was the wedding night switcheroo with Jacob waking up the next morning with Leah instead of Rachel. Laban had promised Rachel to Jacob for his seven years of work but brought Leah to Jacob's tent on his wedding night.

There is no doubt that in this story Jacob was being treated by Laban and Leah exactly how he and his mother,

Rebekah, had treated Esau and Isaac. We might say, "What goes around, comes around." But God was at work here in the life of Jacob. God just taught him a valuable lesson.

This part of the story ends with the words: **"His love for Rachel was greater than his love for Leah"** (Genesis 29:30). I think we can understand why Jacob would love Rachel more than Leah. After all, Jacob was in love with Rachel, not Leah. He wanted to marry Rachel, not Leah. Even so, this was the beginning of Jacob's second major flaw—favoritism.

God's Truth for My Life

1. What is the primary emotion you are feeling about Jacob at this point in the story? Explain why you feel the way you do.

2. Reflect on the marriage customs of Jacob's day. What is positive, negative, unusual, or disturbing to you?

3. Discuss the difference between karma and God's involvement in our lives. (You might want to refer to Pastor Mike's "How Does Grace Change Me?" on page 39).

4. Deception causes a range of emotions. If someone deceived you in the past, what emotions did you experience?

Favoritism 1.0

Remember Zilpah and Bilhah? We've already met these women in a previous chapter. Some of this will be familiar, but I want to give you a few more details. Zilpah was a servant girl whom Laban gave to Leah on the occasion of her becoming Jacob's wife. Bilhah was also a servant girl. Laban gave her to Rachel when she became Jacob's wife.

The marriage of Jacob and Rachel began the same way that Abraham and Sarah's marriage began and Isaac and Rebekah's marriage began. The women were unable to get pregnant. But that wasn't the case with Rachel's sister, Leah. **"When the Lord saw that Leah was not loved, he enabled her to conceive, but Rachel remained childless"** (Genesis 29:31).

The Hebrew word translated into English as "not loved" has a wide range of meanings. On one end of the spectrum, it can mean "loved less." On the other end of the spectrum, it can mean "hated." And, in the middle, it can mean "unloved." No matter what meaning one chooses, from the very start of his marriage to the two sisters, Jacob showed favoritism to Rachel.

God chose to ease the burden of Leah's being unloved by enabling her to get pregnant easily. She gave birth to Jacob's first four sons: Reuben, Simeon, Levi, and Judah. Leah's feeling of being unloved was a defining factor in her life. After the birth of Reuben, we sense Leah's pain: **"She named him Reuben, for she said, 'It is because the Lord has seen my misery. Surely my husband will love me now'"** (Genesis 29:32). The names she gave to her other three sons also expressed her desire to be loved by Jacob.

Although Rachel had the love of Jacob, she wasn't having any of his children. This created jealously toward Leah and a strained relationship with Jacob. She told Jacob: **"'Give me children, or I'll die!' Jacob became angry with her and said, 'Am I in the place of God, who has kept you from having children?'"** (Genesis 30:1,2).

Rachel came up with a plan to address her inability to give Jacob any children:

Then she said, "Here is Bilhah, my servant. Sleep with her so that she can bear children for me and I too can build a family through her."

So she gave him her servant Bilhah as a wife. Jacob slept with her, and she became pregnant and bore him a son. Then Rachel said, "God has vindicated me; he has listened to my plea and given me a son." Because of this she named him Dan. (verses 3-6)

Do Rachel's impatience and scheming remind you of anyone else? How about Abraham and Sarah? Sarah had become impatient with not having a baby. So she offered her servant, Hagar, to sleep with Abraham. Hagar became pregnant and gave birth to Ishmael. We know from Scripture that Sarah's plan caused much grief and heartache for everyone involved.

Rachel's plan was put into motion with Bilhah getting pregnant and having a son. Rachel named him Dan, which means "he (God) has vindicated me." Then Bilhah got pregnant again and gave birth to another son. His name was Naphtali, a name that reminded Rachel of her struggle with Leah.

It appeared at this point that Leah wasn't having any more children. So it was now her turn to punch back at her rival in this marriage. Leah gave her servant, Zilpah, to Jacob as a surrogate wife. "Take that, Rachel!" Zilpah became pregnant and gave birth to a son, Gad, which means "good fortune." Zilpah then gave birth once more; a son by the name of Asher, which means "happy." Leah was happy because it appeared that she was running away with this baby birthing competition!

But the competition wasn't over. It just entered a new phase.

The competition now moved from surrogate births to herbal supplements—mandrakes. The mandrake is a Mediterranean plant that has blue flowers in the winter and poisonous yellow, plumlike fruit in the summer. Many cultures desired this plant because of a belief that it promoted fertility. In ancient Greece, the mandrake root was used as a narcotic. It was used medicinally for anxiety and depression, insomnia, and gout. It was also used as a love potion. It was in Greece that the resemblance of the roots to a human was first recorded.

Mandrakes even show up in the popular Harry Potter book series. Hogwarts students studied mandrakes in Professor Pomona Sprout's herbology class.

What happens next reads like it came from a script for a soap opera:

During wheat harvest, Reuben went out into the fields and found some mandrake plants, which he brought to his mother Leah. Rachel said to Leah, "Please give me some of your son's mandrakes."

But she said to her, "Wasn't it enough that you took away my husband? Will you take my son's mandrakes too?"

"Very well," Rachel said, "he can sleep with you tonight in return for your son's mandrakes."

So when Jacob came in from the fields that evening, Leah went out to meet him. "You must sleep with me," she said. "I have hired you with my son's mandrakes." So he slept with her that night. (Genesis 30:14-16).

Even with the use of mandrakes, Rachel did not get pregnant for many years. But in the meantime, Leah gave birth to three more babies—two sons and a daughter. The sons were named Issachar (meaning "reward") and Zebulun (meaning "honor"). The daughter was named Dinah, a Hebrew word for "judge."

Rachel continued to pray for a child, and God finally answered that prayer in the affirmative. Rachel became pregnant and gave birth to a son. She named him Joseph, which means "may he add." It seemed that in the naming of Joseph, Rachel was asking God to give her another son.

After Joseph was born to Rachel, Jacob approached Laban with the expressed desire to return to his homeland down south. Jacob had completed his required 14 years of service. But Laban convinced him to stay longer, another six years for a total of 20. During those six years, Jacob's flocks grew larger and larger. When we get to the part about Jacob's blessings, we will find out why.

Jacob realized that eventually it was time to leave because Laban's attitude toward him had deteriorated. So one day Jacob, along with his family and servants and flocks, left without telling Laban to return to the land God had promised him.

Sons of Jacob	Meaning of Name	Mother
Reuben	Sounds like the Hebrew for *he has seen my misery*; the name means *see, a son*.	Leah
Simeon	Probably means *one who hears*.	Leah
Levi	Sounds like and may be derived from the Hebrew for *attached*.	Leah
Judah	Sounds like and may be derived from the Hebrew for *praise*.	Leah
Dan	Means *he has vindicated*.	Bilhah (Rachel's servant)
Naphtali	Means *my struggle*.	Bilhah (Rachel's servant)
Gad	Can mean *good fortune*.	Zilpah (Leah's servant)
Asher	Means *happy*.	Zilpah (Leah's servant)
Issachar	Sounds like the Hebrew for *reward*.	Leah
Zebulun	Probably means *honor*.	Leah
Joseph	Means *may he add*.	Rachel
Benjamin	Means *son of my right hand*.	Rachel

There was one more son yet to be born to Rachel, but not for many years to come. Jacob would first finish his 20 years working with Laban and return home to be reunited with Esau. After that reunion, Jacob headed to Bethel. From Bethel, Jacob headed south to see his father, Isaac, at Hebron. On the way, near Bethlehem, Rachel went into labor. Her labor was difficult, and she died giving birth to a son. Rachel had named him Ben-Oni, "son of my distress." Jacob did not accept this name. Instead, Jacob said he would be called Benjamin, "son of my right hand." Benjamin was the last son of Jacob to be born.

With the death of Rachel, there would be no more favoritism shown between Jacob's wives. Jacob's favoritism, however, would find a new focus. It would be directed at the firstborn son of his favorite wife.

Jacob's favoritism would pivot to Joseph.

God's Truth for My Life

1. God intended marriage to consist of one man and one woman. From the lives of Jacob, Rachel, Leah, Bilhah, and Zilpah, what were the many consequences of ignoring God's design for marriage?

2. Jacob's favoritism for Rachel caused undo pain for everyone involved. What was the pain experienced by . . .

   a. Leah?

   b. Rachel?

   c. Bilhah and Zilpah?

   d. Jacob?

3. Have you ever experienced pain from someone showing favoritism either toward you or toward someone else? Share your experience.

4. God can turn human mistakes and misery for his good. What was one benefit resulting from Jacob having a polygamous marriage? (Hint: the number 12.)

Favoritism 2.0

We pick up the story of Jacob and Joseph in Genesis chapter 37. The opening verses describe the favoritism that Jacob (whose name had been changed by God to Israel—more about this in the next chapter).

Jacob lived in the land where his father had stayed, the land of Canaan.

This is the account of Jacob's family line.

Joseph, a young man of seventeen, was tending the flocks with his brothers, the sons of Bilhah and the sons of Zilpah, his father's wives, and he brought their father a bad report about them.

Now Israel loved Joseph more than any of his other sons, because he had been born to him in his old age; and he made an ornate robe for him. When his brothers saw that their father loved him more than any of them, they hated him and could not speak a kind word to him. (verses 1–4)

Joseph, a 17-year-old teenager, helped tend the flocks with his older brothers: Dan, Naphtali, Gad, and Asher (the four sons of the two surrogate wives). It was likely that Joseph had to do the jobs the older, "in charge" brothers didn't want to do.

Something happened out in the fields one day that Joseph felt compelled to report back to his father. Was it insignificant, making Joseph a little tattletale? Or was it more serious, something that Jacob actually needed to know about. We don't know. Either way, his brothers did not appreciate it.

We are told in the biblical text that Jacob loved Joseph more than any of his others sons. It's another example of favoritism. The reason for his special love was because Joseph was born to him in his old age. He was old indeed. Jacob was 91 when Joseph was born.

There was even more favoritism shown when Jacob made an ornate robe for Joseph to wear. We don't know if it was a "technicolor dream coat" (as in the Broadway play), but it was special. The Hebrew word suggests it had sleeves extending to the wrists and a robe that extended to the ankles. This was the kind of robe that royalty wore. It's tough to do manual labor when one is wearing such a long and flowing robe.

The favoritism shown to Joseph created envy and outright hatred for Joseph, so much so that the brothers could not even bring themselves to say the customary greeting of "Shalom" to him.

Joseph didn't do himself any favors by sharing with his brothers two dreams that he had on two different nights. The telling of these dreams only inflamed the brothers' hatred of Joseph.

Joseph had a dream, and when he told it to his brothers, they hated him all the more. He said to them, "Listen to this dream I had: We were binding sheaves of grain out in the field when suddenly my sheaf rose and stood upright, while your sheaves gathered around mine and bowed down to it."

His brothers said to him, "Do you intend to reign over us? Will you actually rule us?" And they hated him all the more because of his dream and what he had said.

Then he had another dream, and he told it to his brothers. "Listen," he said, "I had another dream, and this time the sun and moon and eleven stars were bowing down to me."

When he told his father as well as his brothers, his father rebuked him and said, "What is this dream you had? Will your mother and I and your brothers actually come and bow down to the ground before you?" His brothers were jealous of him, but his father kept the matter in mind. (Genesis 37:5-11)

The first dream pictured the brothers bowing down to Joseph. The second dream pictured the same except that Joseph's father and mother would bow down as well. Jacob questioned Joseph about this dream, but he also tucked it away in the back of his memory. Because of the dreams, the brothers just hated Joseph all the more. It became so intense that they decided to kill their younger brother.

One day Jacob told Joseph to go and see how his brothers were doing tending the flocks. This time some of the older brothers were there. Reuben and Judah are two that are mentioned, both sons of Leah.

So Joseph went after his brothers and found them near Dothan. But they saw him in the distance, and before he reached them, they plotted to kill him.

"Here comes that dreamer!" they said to each other. "Come now, let's kill him and throw him into one of these cisterns and say that a ferocious animal devoured him. Then we'll see what comes of his dreams." (Genesis 37:17-20)

When Reuben (the oldest brother) heard about the plan, he suggested not killing Joseph but just leaving him in the cistern. Reuben had the idea of circling back and rescuing Joseph from the cistern and taking him back to his father.

When Joseph arrived, the brothers stripped him of his robe and threw him into the cistern. Then they sat down to have lunch. Imagine that! Throw your brother into a cistern to die and then sit down to have some lunch! As they were eating, a caravan came by. Judah suggested a change of plans. The brothers decided not to kill their brother but rather sold him to some Ishmaelites, also known as Midianites, who took Joseph with them to Egypt.

There was an additional act of lies and deception that we learn about. It is one that Joseph's brothers inflicted upon their father.

Then they got Joseph's robe, slaughtered a goat and dipped the robe in the blood. They took the ornate robe back to their father and said, "We found this. Examine it to see whether it is your son's robe."

He recognized it and said, "It is my son's robe! Some ferocious animal has devoured him. Joseph has surely been torn to pieces."

Then Jacob tore his clothes, put on sackcloth and mourned for his son many days. All his sons and daughters came to comfort him, but he refused to be comforted. "No," he said, "I will continue to mourn until I join my son in the grave." So his father wept for him.

Meanwhile, the Midianites sold Joseph in Egypt to

Potiphar, one of Pharaoh's officials, the captain of the guard. (Genesis 37:31-36)

The deception on their father was the spoiled fruit of their hatred for Joseph. That hatred had been ignited by a flame of favoritism on the part of their father, Jacob. Deception and favoritism—the two major flaws in this patriarchal family; flaws that passed from one generation to the next.

God's Truth for My Life

1. The default position, even as Christians, is that we want to control our lives. So we cheat, lie, and fuel family tension. Where do you see these flaws in your life, and how do you deal with them?

2. From our study of these Old Testament patriarchs, it becomes clear that the flaws of the parents oftentimes show up in their children. Discuss how we, as Christians, can break the cycle.

3. C. S. Lewis once wrote: "Envy is insatiable. The more you concede to it, the more it will demand." Discuss how this quote relates to our study of Jacob and his family.

Blessing Upon Blessing

Bruce Becker

I mentioned previously that God initiated a spiritual training program for Jacob. It started right after Jacob had stolen the birthright blessing and then fled from his brother, who wanted to kill him. This training program would bring to Jacob blessing upon blessing.

Up until now, we've only looked at the flaws of Jacob, his parents, and his siblings. We might be tempted to ask, "Why would God want to bless such a messed-up family?" Well, that's the thing about the Lord, the God of free and faithful grace. He loves the unlovable, and he chooses to bless bad people.

Spending 20 years with his Uncle Laban was part of this training program. Laban was so much like Jacob. He was deceptive. He didn't play fair. He was only interested in what benefitted him. In those two decades of life with Laban, God taught Jacob some hard but valuable lessons.

But the most significant part of Jacob's spiritual training program came from Jacob's seven encounters with God himself. Let's take a look at them and learn how God delivered blessing upon blessing to Jacob and to us.

Jacob's First Encounter With God

In 1971 the British rock band Led Zeppelin released a hit song entitled "Stairway to Heaven." Pastor Mike referred to it earlier. The song was about materialism and greed. The lead singer, Robert Plant, claimed that it was specifically about a woman getting everything she wanted without giving anything back.

This song has absolutely nothing to do with Jacob's first encounter with God. And yet, it has *everything* to do with it. Before this first encounter, Jacob was all about materialism, greed, and getting everything he wanted without giving anything back. That was about to change when Jacob encountered his own stairway to heaven.

In "Is God Here?" Pastor Mike told the story of what happened a few days after Jacob fled for his life. One night he arrived at a "certain place."

As Pastor Mike described it, that night Jacob had a vision of a stairway to heaven with angels ascending and descending upon it.

The Hebrew word translated as "stairway" can also be translated as "ladder" or "ramp." We don't know for sure what it looked like. In my mind (probably influenced by Sunday school artwork), I picture it as a wide, stone staircase. But that's just me. What's important is that this stairway went from earth to heaven. Jacob could not have missed the significance of this, namely, that the God of heaven is involved with what is happening on earth. God is here. And the angels ascending to heaven and descending to earth indicated that they were carrying out the will of God on this earth.

When Jacob laid down to sleep, he was concerned only with escaping Esau's threats and getting to a place of safety among his Uncle Laban's clan. He could not have expected an encounter with God himself. God, in his love and mercy, took the initiative. He reached out and revealed himself to Jacob.

What amazing promises God made to Jacob! There were no conditions, no prerequisites, no stipulations, no quid pro quos. Just one-way promises made by the God of free and faithful grace to a heal-grabbing fugitive who, frankly, did not deserve a thing. But that's just like our God. He wants to bless us.

These were promises that mirrored the promises that God had made to Abraham and Isaac. They also mirrored the second blessing (the not-stolen one) that Isaac pronounced on Jacob before he left Beersheba. Jacob was now the third generation to hear these promises of God. It is through Jacob that the promised Messiah, the Christ, the Son of the living God, would one day come to this earth.

Are you struck by the scope and specificity of God's promises? I am.

- "Jacob, you and your descendants will inhabit the very ground on which you are sleeping."
- "Jacob, your descendants will be as numerous as the dust of the earth."
- "Jacob, all peoples on the earth will be blessed through you and your descendants."
- "Jacob, I will bring you back to this place."
- "Jacob, I will not leave you."

In this list, it is God's third promise that is so comforting for you and me and for all the other people who aren't part of the gene pool of Abraham, Isaac, and Jacob. Through Jacob's "greatest descendant," God has chosen to bless us. That greatest descendant is Jesus. With Jesus' life, death, resurrection, and ascension, we have received blessing upon blessing.

When Jacob awoke from his sleep, he responded in a way that revealed a different heart than the one we've seen up until this point. He acknowledged God's presence, named the place Bethel (house of God), and made a confession of faith, vowing to worship the God at the top of the stairs.

The grace that God showed to Jacob was undeserved and unexpected. Instead of giving Jacob what he actually deserved, God instead gave him his promised blessings. But just as God's grace wasn't just for Jacob, neither are God's blessings. God's grace is intended for all people, you and me included. When God's grace touches our lives, the result is blessing upon blessing.

God's Truth for My Life

1. How do you picture the stairway to heaven in Jacob's dream?

2. Jacob's encounter with God was a significant part of his spiritual training program. What surprises you the most about his encounter with God? When or where have you encountered God yourself?

3. List two or three results of this spiritual training lesson for Jacob's life. What spiritual training lessons have you received from God in your life?

4. Author and theologian Frederick Buechner wrote the following in reference to Jacob: "God doesn't love people for who they are, but for who God is." What does this statement say to you? Would you say it any differently? If so, how?

Jacob's Second and Third Encounters With God

Jacob's second encounter with God happened, according to Jacob, during a breeding season. We aren't told exactly when this happened. Was it the previous one? Was it five years earlier? We don't know. Whenever it was, God came to Jacob again in a dream. Jacob shared the content of that dream with Rachel and Leah after God had likely encountered him a third time. This is a bit confusing, I know. Let me explain.

Jacob's third encounter with God occurred 20 years after his first encounter. It occurred as tensions between Laban's clan and Jacob's clan were escalating. Genesis chapter 31 begins:

> **Jacob heard that Laban's sons were saying, "Jacob has taken everything our father owned and has gained all this wealth from what belonged to our father." And Jacob noticed that Laban's attitude toward him was not what it had been.**
>
> **Then the Lord said to Jacob, "Go back to the land of your fathers and to your relatives, and I will be with you."** (verses 1–3)

This was the third encounter. It was very brief, but very specific—"It's time to leave." As a result of this encounter with God, **"Jacob sent word to Rachel and Leah to come out to the fields where his flocks were"** (Genesis 31:4).

When Rachel and Leah came out to the fields, Jacob explained a few things as he prepared to tell them what the Lord had directed him to do. They were to return to the place where he was born, to go back to the land of Canaan. Jacob told Rachel and Leah about the deteriorating attitude that Laban had toward him. He explained that, although he had worked hard for their father, Laban continually cheated him. Ten different times Laban had changed his wages, but God did not allow any harm to come to him. Just the opposite. Jacob went on to explain:

> **"If he** [Laban] **said, 'The speckled ones will be your wages,' then all the flocks gave birth to speckled young; and if he said, 'The streaked ones will be your wages,' then all the flocks bore streaked young. So God has taken away your father's livestock and has given them to me."** (Genesis 31:8,9)

It is in this conversation with Rachel and Leah that Jacob explained what seems to be the second encounter he had with God:

> **"In breeding season I once had a dream in which I looked up and saw that the male goats mating with the flock were streaked, speckled or spotted. The angel of God said to me in the dream, 'Jacob.' I answered, 'Here I am.' And he said, 'Look up and see that all the male goats mating with the flock are streaked, speckled or spotted, for I have seen all that Laban has been doing to you. I am the God of Bethel, where you anointed a pillar and where you made a vow to me. Now leave this land at once and go back to your native land.'"** (Genesis 31:10-13)

Some Bible scholars believe that these were not two different encounters that Jacob had with God but one in the same. It seems, though, that the breeding season encounter occurred in the past and the brief directive from the Lord to return home was in real time in this account. Either way, the message from God is the same: "It's time to leave."

The breeding season encounter with God revealed what God had been up to in the previous six years of Jacob's life and work. He was working to bless Jacob, and the angel of God tells us how he did it.

Laban had been trying to take advantage of Jacob. When it comes to goats, apparently streaked, speckled, or spotted goats were less common than solid color goats. Those were the goats that Laban decided were Jacob's wages in order to keep Jacob's flocks smaller than his own. However, it didn't work out that way. God got directly involved because of Laban's cheating schemes. God saw to it that the male goats would mate with the "triple S" goats (streaked, speckled, and spotted). This resulted in Jacob's herds growing larger and Laban's herds growing smaller.

God was working to bless Jacob.

Jacob seemed to have had a concern that his sister wives, Rachel and Leah, would not want to leave the home they grew up in. Rachel and Leah's response to what Jacob had told them may have come as a surprise. Rachel and Leah had a different yet also unfavorable perspective on their father:

> **Then Rachel and Leah replied, "Do we still have any share in the inheritance of our father's estate? Does he not regard us as foreigners? Not only has he sold us, but he has used up what was paid for us. Surely all the wealth that God took away from our father belongs to us and our children. So do whatever God has told you."** (Genesis 31:14-16)

From Rachel and Leah's perspective, their father had treated them like property rather than as dearly loved daughters. What Rachel and Leah were referring to was the bridal dowry. This was the gift that the groom paid to his father-in-law in order to marry his daughter (in this case daughters). It seemed that Rachel and Leah expected that at least a portion of Jacob's dowry (14 years of labor to Laban) should be theirs. A dowry was like an insurance policy in case something happened to the husband. But Laban kept the dowry for himself and used it up. Rachel and Leah were feeling more like commodities that their father sold to Jacob rather than flesh-and-blood daughters. As a result, they were more than willing to leave with Jacob. Laban's deception and fraud perpetrated against Jacob was about to cost him his own daughters.

The breeding season encounter was an important reminder of God's promises to Jacob. He had promised to bless Jacob, and this was another way that he had.

For us, we ought not to underestimate God's involvement in our lives and in this world's affairs. Like the dream Jacob had of the stairway to heaven that portrayed God's involvement in his life, God got involved in the everyday mating activity of goats in order to bless Jacob with flocks and wealth. It's another reminder that God provides blessing upon blessing.

God's Truth for My Life

1. Have you ever experienced God's nudging of you to go in a certain direction in life or to make a decision one way or another? Share your experience.

2. When it comes to making big decisions in my family, we have regularly prayed the following: "Dear Lord, if this is not a decision that will be a blessing to us, then we pray that you would prevent it from happening." Have you ever prayed a prayer like that? If so, what can you share about how God answered it?

3. Laban's deception and greed had consequences. Can you share any experiences from your life or the lives of others that were similar?

4. Have you ever experienced consequences from your actions? How did God still bless you?

Jacob's Fourth Encounter With God

At God's directive, Jacob packed up and left Harran with his wives, children, servants, cows, sheep and goats, camels, donkeys, and all of their possessions. They left, however, without telling Laban.

Laban learned of Jacob's exodus three days later (Laban had previously put three days' distance between his flocks and Jacob's because he didn't trust Jacob) and immediately went after them. After a week, he finally caught up to Jacob's caravan. By the way, God had come to Laban in a dream warning him not to say anything to Jacob, either good or bad. Who knows what Laban might have done without God's warning of judgment?

Genesis chapter 31 records the dialogue of that meeting: the self-righteous tirade of Laban, Jacob's legitimate charges against Laban's deceptive and greedy treatment of him, Laban's accusation that Jacob stole his idols (Rachel actually took them), and the eventual peaceful agreement and separation between Jacob and Laban. This chapter in Genesis is worth a read, but for our purposes, we want to move ahead to Jacob's fourth encounter with God.

Jacob and his caravan continued to travel south toward the land of Canaan. They traveled along the eastern side of the Jordan River to the Jabbok River, an east/west tributary that flowed into the Jordan. As Jacob approached the Jabbok River, angels came to meet him. When Jacob saw them, he said, **"'This is the camp of God!' So he named that place Mahanaim"** (Genesis 32:2).

Do you recall a previous time when Jacob witnessed angels? It was 20 years earlier at Bethel, shortly after Jacob fled his home. It was in the dream of the stairway to heaven on which angels were ascending and descending. Jacob was blessed by God to see angels when he left and now again when he returned. They were a reminder that God was with him.

At some time during the previous two decades, Esau left his father's home in Beersheba and went to occupy the Kingdom of Edom. Isaac had moved as well. He went to live in Hebron.

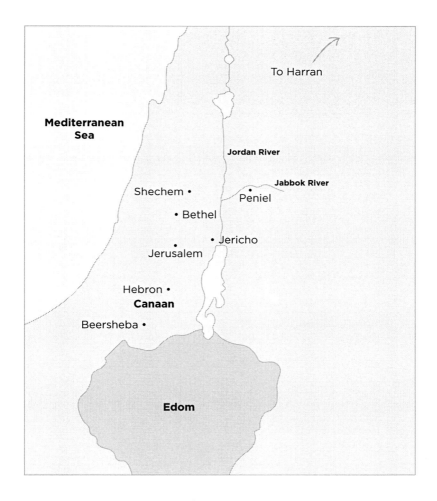

The next step in Jacob's plan to reunite with his brother was to send messengers to Esau:

Jacob sent messengers ahead of him to his brother Esau in the land of Seir, the country of Edom. He instructed them: "This is what you are to say to my lord Esau: 'Your servant Jacob says, I have been staying with Laban and have remained there till now. I have cattle and donkeys, sheep and goats, male and female servants. Now I am sending this message to my lord, that I may find favor in your eyes.'" (Genesis 32:3–5)

There are several things in Jacob's message to Esau that stand out. "Your servant Jacob" and ". . . sending this message to my lord" are words that give honor and respect to Esau as the older brother. "That I may find favor in your eyes" was Jacob revealing his desire to be reconciled with his brother. Jacob was sending the message that he was no longer interested or in need of the double portion of the birthright blessing he stole.

When the messengers returned, they reported, **"We went to your brother Esau, and now he is coming to meet you, and four hundred men are with him"** (Genesis 32:6). Yikes!

Upon receiving this report, Jacob immediately did two things. First, he put together a plan to minimize his losses in the event that Esau was coming for revenge. Second, he went to God in prayer.

The plan was simple. Jacob divided all of his people, his flocks, herds, and camels into two groups. If Esau attacked one group, the other might be able to escape.

The prayer was incredible. It included Jacob reminding God of his promises and directives for him to do exactly what he was doing. Jacob acknowledged that he was unworthy of God's blessings. He prayed for safety for himself and his family and acknowledged his inability to handle this situation on his own. He reminded God a second time of his promises:

> **"O God of my father Abraham, God of my father Isaac, LORD, you who said to me, 'Go back to your country and your relatives, and I will make you prosper,' I am unworthy of all the kindness and faithfulness you have shown your servant. I had only my staff when I crossed this Jordan, but now I have become two camps. Save me, I pray, from the hand of my brother Esau, for I am afraid he will come and attack me, and also the mothers with their children. But you have said, 'I will surely make you prosper and will make your descendants like the sand of the sea, which cannot be counted.'"**
> (Genesis 32:9–12)

There was one more thing to do before Esau would arrive. Jacob sent a gift to his brother Esau:

- 200 female goats and 20 male goats
- 200 ewes and 20 rams
- 30 female camels with their young
- 40 cows and 10 bulls
- 20 female donkeys and 10 male donkeys

That's no small gift!

Jacob instructed his servants to keep each herd separate and to keep space between each herd. The servants headed out to meet Esau. Jacob remained behind in the camp.

It was that night that Jacob had his fourth encounter with God, which turned into a wrestling match. There are some aspects of this encounter between Jacob and God that are easy to understand and others that are not.

What is clear is that Jacob struggled with God all night, both spiritually and physically. As daylight approached, God decided to end the struggle. He did it merely by touching Jacob's hip and throwing the entire hip socket out of joint. God could have done this at any time, but he wanted the struggle to continue all night. Once Jacob's hip was out of joint, he was unable physically to continue the struggle. Yet he continued to hold on to his opponent.

When his opponent told Jacob to let go, he refused: **"I will not let you go unless you bless me"** (Genesis 32:26). This was huge! God delights in our bold requests to receive his blessings. We should never hold back in asking for them. God had promised to bless Jacob

God delights in our bold requests.

so that he could be a blessing to others. Jacob boldly asked that God make good on his promise.

God asked Jacob what his name was. Obviously, the question wasn't needed for God's sake, as though he forgot, but rather for Jacob's sake. "My name is Jacob, the heel grabber who took advantage of others." God responded, **"Your name will no longer be Jacob, but Israel, because you have struggled with God and with humans and have overcome"** (Genesis 32:28).

In ancient times, when a person acquired a new name, it was because there was change in the person's identity. The man who left 20 years earlier as a heel-grabbing deceiver had returned as Israel, one who wrestled with God and had overcome. Jacob now embraced God's promises and his blessings—blessing upon blessing.

Jacob was now ready to meet his brother Esau.

Jacob looked up and there was Esau, coming with his four hundred men; so he divided the children among Leah, Rachel and the two female servants. He put the female servants and their children in front, Leah and her children next, and Rachel and Joseph in the rear. He himself went on ahead and bowed down to the ground seven times as he approached his brother.

But Esau ran to meet Jacob and embraced him; he threw his arms around his neck and kissed him. And they wept. (Genesis 33:1-4)

On the previous pages, we've observed how God changed the heart of Jacob. And we know that only God can change hearts. At this reunion of brothers, we see that Esau's heart was changed as well. We don't know the details of how God changed his heart, but he did.

It's more evidence that God graciously provided blessing upon blessing for both Jacob and Esau.

God's Truth for My Life

1. Although Jacob had his reasons for leaving Harran without telling Laban, why would it have been better for him to have a face-to-face conversation?

2. When Jacob heard that Esau was coming with four hundred men, he made a plan. Did he not trust God? Was he relying on himself? Where do trusting God and making practical plans intersect?

3. When Jacob wrestled with God, he would not let God go until God blessed him. Evaluate your prayer life in terms of how persistent you are in wrestling for God's blessings.

4. What comfort do you have in your heart after thinking through this encounter between God and Jacob?

Jacob's Fifth Encounter With God

Although it looked as though Jacob's spiritual training program was complete, he had two additional encounters with God when he returned to Canaan. Both of these encounters were focused on reinforcing what God had already said and done for Jacob. **"Then God said to Jacob, 'Go up to Bethel and settle there, and build an altar there to God, who appeared to you when you were fleeing from your brother Esau'"** (Genesis 35:1). This fifth encounter occurred near Shechem. Jacob bought a plot of ground near the city so that he had a place to pitch his tent and set up an altar to God. He called it El Elohe Israel ("mighty is the God of Israel").

Before leaving, Jacob did something that again reflected that he was a changed man: **"So Jacob said to his household and to all who were with him, 'Get rid of the foreign gods you have with you, and purify yourselves and change your clothes'"** (Genesis 35:2).

Recall when Jacob's caravan left Harran without informing Laban and Laban went after them. One of the issues Laban was angry about was that someone had stolen his household gods, or idols. Laban assumed it was Jacob. When accused, Jacob made a rash statement that could have cost his wife Rachel her life: **"'But if you find anyone who has your gods, that person shall not live. In the presence of our relatives, see for yourself whether there is anything of yours here with me; and if so, take it.' Now Jacob did not know that Rachel had stolen the gods"** (Genesis 31:32).

Laban made a search for his treasured idols but did not find them. That was because they were in Rachel's camel's pack saddle. She was essentially sitting on them. She did not dismount from her camel, offering the excuse that it was the time of her monthly menstrual period.

We aren't told why Rachel took these household idols. Perhaps it was revenge upon her greedy father, taking something that he treasured. It would have been revenge for his taking something she treasured, namely her marriage to Jacob that had to be shared with her sister and her bridal dowry. Or perhaps Rachel wasn't a worshiper of just one God, believing that other gods existed. Or perhaps she didn't want her father worshiping idols, so she took them. We aren't told.

Jacob knew that there were idols in the luggage of his clan. He wanted them gone. He wanted his clan to worship the true God only. **"So they gave Jacob all the foreign gods they had and the rings in their ears, and Jacob buried them under the oak at Shechem. Then they set out, and the terror of God fell on the towns all around them so that no one pursued them"** (Genesis 35:4,5).

With the spiritual housekeeping complete, Jacob's caravan headed to Bethel to settle there. We might have expected Jacob to go see his father, Isaac, next. Returning to Bethel first must have been very important to Jacob. The distance between Shechem and Bethel was only about 20 miles. **"There he built an altar, and he called the place El Bethel, because it was there that God revealed himself to him when he was fleeing from his brother"** (Genesis 35:7).

God blessed Jacob at Bethel once before. Now he blessed Israel there again.

God's Truth for My Life

1. Why do you think God wanted Jacob to return to Bethel even before going to see his father? What does that indicate about Jacob's priorities? What do Jacob's actions say to you?

2. God is a jealous God. He wants to be the only God in our lives. We don't have idols that we keep in our homes, or do we? What are some of the idols in your life that compete with your relationship with Jesus?

Jacob's Sixth Encounter With God

The sixth encounter that Jacob had with God occurred after he arrived in Bethel. There God repeated Jacob's name change and the blessings that God had given at Bethel the first time:

> **God appeared to him again and blessed him. God said to him, "Your name is Jacob, but you will no longer be called Jacob; your name will be Israel." So he named him Israel.**

> **And God said to him, "I am God Almighty; be fruitful and increase in number. A nation and a community of nations will come from you, and kings will be among your descendants. The land I gave to Abraham and Isaac I also give to you, and I will give this land to your descendants after you."**
> (Genesis 35:9-12)

When Jacob encountered God at Bethel the first time (after fleeing from Esau), he took the stone that he had used as a pillow and set it upright and poured oil on it. After arriving at Bethel from Shechem, Jacob built an altar there. Now after this sixth encounter, **"Jacob set up a stone pillar at the place where God had talked with him . . . he also poured oil on it"** (Genesis 35:14). Stone, altar, and now pillar—each commemorating an encounter with God.

The Lord renewed his covenant promise with Jacob at Bethel. From the first time Jacob was at Bethel until this time, God had provided Jacob with his spiritual training. Jacob had come full circle as a man and as a believer in the God of free and faithful grace.

With this covenant renewal completed, Jacob and his clan headed south toward Jerusalem. Somewhere just south of Jerusalem, Rachel went into labor and gave birth to her son Benjamin. During childbirth, however, she died. Jacob buried her along the road between Jerusalem and Bethlehem and erected a pillar to mark her grave.

From Bethlehem Jacob's caravan headed south to Hebron, where Isaac lived. Jacob would enjoy the next dozen years with his father before Isaac died at the age of 180.

Jacob and Esau buried their father in the tomb at Machpelah in Hebron. Abraham had originally purchased this property as a place to bury his wife, Sarah. Buried there were Abraham, Sarah, Rebekah, and now Isaac. In the future Leah would be buried there as well as Jacob. The tomb still exists today. It is called the Cave of the Patriarchs.

God's Truth for My Life

1. Why do you think God repeated Jacob's name change and his promised blessings? What does that teach you about the blessings God has promised to you?

2. Jacob had a name change. In what sense have you had your name changed as well?

Jacob's (Israel's) Seventh Encounter With God

When he buried his father, Isaac, Jacob was 120 years old. His next and final encounter with God wouldn't happen for another decade. What took place in those ten years could be its own book. But let's at least identify the major events in those ten years that led up to Jacob's seventh encounter with God. This is the story of Jacob's son Joseph. Everything that happened in Joseph's life was preparation for how God was planning to keep his promises.

As you read through this timeline of Joseph's life, stop and ponder the flaws, the tragedies, and the blessings that were part of Joseph's life.

Favoritism and Sibling Rivalry

- Jacob and his clan lived in Hebron, south of Jerusalem and west of the Dead Sea.

- Jacob loved Joseph more than his other sons because he was born to him in his old age.

- Jacob showed favoritism to Joseph by giving him a special robe to wear. This created jealousy among his brothers.

- Joseph shared his dreams with his brothers and parents. They were dreams in which all family members bowed down to Joseph. These dreams fostered hatred among the brothers.

- The brothers planned to kill Joseph but instead sold him to merchants who were traveling nearby on their way to Egypt.

Joseph's Ups and Downs in Egypt

- When they arrived in Egypt, the merchants sold Joseph

to Potiphar, one of Pharaoh's officials who was the captain of the guard.

- Potiphar put Joseph in charge of his entire household because Potiphar realized that the Lord blessed everything Joseph did.
- Potiphar's wife repeatedly tried to seduce Joseph. In one attempt, she grabbed his cloak and Joseph ran out of the house without it.
- Potiphar's wife accused Joseph of trying to seduce her. Potiphar had Joseph thrown into prison.
- The Lord blessed Joseph in prison. The warden put Joseph in charge of all the prisoners.
- One day, two new prisoners arrived, Pharaoh's cupbearer and baker. Pharaoh was angry with them. The warden assigned them to Joseph.
- That same night both the cupbearer and the baker had dreams, but neither knew what they meant.
- Joseph, acknowledging that dream interpretation belonged to God, interpreted the dreams—the cupbearer would get his job back; the baker would be put to death.

Joseph's Rise to Power in Egypt
- Two years later, Pharaoh had dreams that no one could interpret. The cupbearer remembered Joseph and told his story. Pharaoh sent for Joseph.
- Joseph stated to Pharaoh that God would interpret his dreams. Both dreams meant that Egypt would have seven years of abundance and then seven years of famine.
- Joseph recommended a plan to Pharaoh to deal with this. Pharaoh put Joseph in charge. Joseph became the second most powerful person in Egypt at just 30 years old.

- Joseph's plan was to store up grain during the years of abundance so that it could be sold during the years of the famine.

- Joseph married and had two sons, Manasseh and Ephraim.

Joseph Reunited With His Brothers

- **"When Jacob learned that there was grain in Egypt, he said to his sons . . . 'Go down there and buy some for us'"** (Genesis 42:1,2).

- When the brothers arrived, they met Joseph and bowed down to him. Joseph recognized them, but the brothers did not recognize Joseph.

- Joseph inquired about their family. The brothers indicated 1 of the 12 sons was at home with their father and 1 son "was no more."

- Joseph accused them of being spies and determined that one of the brothers (Simeon) needed to stay in Egypt until the rest would return along with the youngest brother, Benjamin.

- Joseph had the silver, which was used to pay for the grain, secretly put back into the brothers' grain sacks.

- The brothers returned and told Jacob all that had happened. Jacob was filled with grief because he feared losing Benjamin along with Joseph and Simeon.

- When the grain ran out, Jacob told his sons to go to Egypt and buy more. Reluctantly, with assurances of Benjamin's safety from Reuben and Judah, Jacob allowed Benjamin to go with them.

- When they arrived in Egypt and Joseph saw Benjamin with them, he told his servant to bring them to his house and prepare a meal for them.

- Joseph gave seating instructions to his servant, seating them from the oldest to the youngest. The brothers were amazed. Joseph also instructed that Benjamin receive a double portion of food.

- Joseph instructed his servants to put his own silver cup in the grain bag that belonged to Benjamin. The brothers began the journey home.

- Joseph then told his servants to go after the brothers and bring them back because Benjamin "stole" Joseph's cup.

- When the brothers stood before Joseph, he stated that only the one who had the cup in his bag would become his slave. The rest could return home.

- The brothers pleaded with Joseph to allow Benjamin to return otherwise their father would die in misery.

Joseph Reveals Himself to His Brothers

- Joseph finally revealed himself to his brothers: **"'I am Joseph! Is my father still living?' But his brothers were not able to answer him, because they were terrified at his presence. Then Joseph said to his brothers, 'Come close to me.' When they had done so, he said, 'I am your brother Joseph, the one you sold into Egypt! And now, do not be distressed and do not be angry with yourselves for selling me here, because it was to save lives that God sent me ahead of you. For two years now there has been famine in the land, and for the next five years there will be no plowing and reaping. But God sent me ahead of you to preserve for you a remnant on earth and to save your lives by a great deliverance'"** (Genesis 45:3-7).

Jacob's Entire Clan Moves to Egypt

- After an emotional reunion, Joseph directed his brothers to return home. Then Joseph told them to bring their father and his entire clan to Egypt to live.
- When Jacob and his clan of 70 people set out for Egypt, they stopped at Beersheba where Jacob offered sacrifices to the God of his father Isaac.

That night, Jacob experienced his seventh encounter with God:

God spoke to Israel in a vision at night and said, "Jacob! Jacob!"

"Here I am," he replied.

"I am God, the God of your father," he said. "Do not be afraid to go down to Egypt, for I will make you into a great nation there. I will go down to Egypt with you, and I will surely bring you back again. And Joseph's own hand will close your eyes." (Genesis 46:2-4)

God repeated his promise that Jacob's descendants would become a great nation. God would build that nation in the land of Egypt, in a region known as Goshen. God also assured Jacob that his descendants would one day return to the land of promise. By the time they would leave Egypt under the leadership of Moses, they would become a great nation of 600,000 men, not counting women and children. But that wouldn't occur for another 430 years.

Then Jacob left Beersheba, and Israel's sons took their father Jacob and their children and their wives in the carts that Pharaoh had sent to transport him. So Jacob and all his offspring went to Egypt, taking with them their livestock and the possessions they had acquired in Canaan. Jacob brought with him to Egypt his sons and grandsons and his daughters and granddaughters—all his offspring. (Genesis 46:5-7)

Jacob would live with his family in Egypt for 17 more years. Before he died, he requested that he would be buried in the tomb of his fathers at Machpelah in Hebron. The brothers did as their father requested. It brought an end to Jacob's life, a life of blessing upon blessing.

God's Truth for My Life

1. What changes occurred in the heart of Joseph toward his brothers from the time he was 17 until their reunion in Egypt? Over the course of your life, has God changed your heart? In what way?

2. What changes occurred in the hearts of the brothers toward Joseph? Can you identify any changes that have occurred in your heart or those of your siblings?

3. What promises did God repeat to Jacob in his seventh encounter with him? What does this tell us about our God?

Conclusion

Bruce Becker

Flawed but blessed is how we can describe the life of Jacob. Jacob and his family did not have model marriages or perfect parenting or selfless siblings. They were all flawed. And so are we.

But that's not what the Bible's story of Jacob's family is all about. Rather, it is about God's grace and blessing, his plan and his promises. The story is about God's plan and promise to send the world a Savior. The story of Jacob is really about Jesus.

In the Garden of Eden, after the first couple disobeyed their Creator, God came alongside of them with a promise that one of their descendants would restore the perfect relationship between God and mankind. That would be Jesus, God's Son. He would redeem that which had been lost.

With Abraham, Isaac, and Jacob, God promised they would become a great nation and through their descendants all nations on the earth would be blessed. Everything in the Old Testament pointed ahead to Jesus, who would come and change people's lives and eternities.

The story of Jacob shows us clearly that God was, is, and always will be in control of the events of this world. Jacob's dream of the stairway to heaven convinces us of that. God shapes events to accomplish his purposes and to achieve his plans. How else does a 17-year-old slave become the number-two ruler in all of Egypt and save tens of thousands of people's lives, including Jacob's family, from a famine?

GOD is here, and he is in control.

Jacob, you, and me may be flawed, but we are all the more incredibly blessed by a God who loves us with an everlasting love.

God wants to give us blessing upon blessing. Jacob's life is proof of it.

About the Writers

Pastor Mike Novotny has served God's people in full-time ministry since 2007 in Madison and, most recently, at The CORE in Appleton, Wisconsin. He also serves as the lead speaker for Time of Grace, where he shares the good news about Jesus through television, print, and online platforms. Mike loves seeing people grasp the depth of God's amazing grace and unstoppable mercy. His wife continues to love him (despite plenty of reasons not to), and his two daughters open his eyes to the love of God for every Christian. When not talking about Jesus or dating his wife/girls, Mike loves playing soccer, running, and reading.

Dr. Bruce Becker currently serves as the executive vice president for Time of Grace. He is also a respected and well-known church consultant, presenter, advisor, podcaster, and author. He has served as lead pastor of two congregations; as a member of several boards; and on many commissions, committees, and task forces. In 2012 he completed his professional doctorate in leadership and ministry management. Bruce and his wife, Linda, live in Jackson, Wisconsin.

About Time of Grace

Time of Grace is an independent, donor-funded ministry that connects people to God's grace—his love, glory, and power—so they realize the temporary things of life don't satisfy. What brings satisfaction is knowing that because Jesus lived, died, and rose for all of us, we have access to the eternal God—right now and forever.

To discover more, please visit timeofgrace.org or call 800.661.3311.

Help share God's message of grace!

Every gift you give helps Time of Grace reach people around the world with the good news of Jesus. Your generosity and prayer support take the gospel of grace to others through our ministry outreach and help them experience a satisfied life as they see God all around them.

Give today at timeofgrace.org/give or by calling 800.661.3311.

Thank you!